BIG ENGLISH 4

Mario Herrera
Christopher Sol Cruz

PUPIL'S BOOK

Contents

CLIL	Writing	Phonics	I can...
Science: Twins, triplets and quadruplets birth, common, fraternal, identical, quadruplets, rare, triplets, twins **Project:** Famous Twins poster	Parts of a Paragraph	**ear, air** dear, ear, fear, hear, year chair, fair, hair, pair, stairs	...make comparisons. ...describe people. ...talk about twins, triplets and quadruplets. ...write a paragraph.
Social Science: Advertising advert, attractive, believe, company, popular, remember, tool **Project:** Advert	Sequence Words	**ir, ur** bird, girl, sir, shirt, skirt curl, fur, hurt, surf, turn	...talk about what people are doing and where they are going at different times. ...say how often people do things. ...talk about adverts and how they work.
Science: Healthy eating balanced, dairy, diet, grains, guide **Project:** Healthy Eating leaflet	Conjunctions: *because* and *so*	**le, el, al, il** apple, bubble, uncle camel, towel, travel local, medal, sandals April, pencil, pupil	...talk about what people eat. ...make polite requests. ...talk about a balanced diet. ...find and use *because* and *so*.
Science: Germs bacteria, enemies, fungi, germs, microscope, nutrients, poisons, protozoa, toxins, viruses **Project:** Protect Yourself checklist	Using Commas	**kn, wr** knee, knight, knock, knot, know wrap, wreck, wrist, write, wrong	...talk about illnesses and health problems. ...give advice. ...talk about different kinds of germs. ...use commas correctly.
Science: Endangered animals bamboo, burn, centimetre (cm), extinct, moss, pond, stream, wild China, Egypt, Mexico, Myanmar, Nepal, Thailand **Project:** Endangered Animal fact file	End Marks	**ph, wh** dolphin, elephant, phantom, phone, photo whale, wheat, wheel, when, white	...talk about different kinds of animals. ...say why certain animals are endangered. ...use end marks correctly.
Maths: Multiplication average speed, distance travelled, equation, kilometres per hour (km/h), number of hours, times (x) **Project:** Speed poster	Speech Marks	**ge, dge** age, cage, large, page, sponge badge, bridge, edge, fridge, hedge	...talk about the past and the present. ...talk about what people used to do. ...calculate average speed. ...use speech marks correctly.
Geography: World festivals celebrate, feast, fight, glacier, guests, messy, powder **Project:** Unusual Festival poster	Emails	**ue, u_e, ure** blue, glue, true cube, cute, duke, huge nature, picture, treasure	...talk about special days and traditions. ...talk about dates. ...talk about world festivals. ...write an email.
History: Hobbies from the past croquet, employer, fabric, marbles, needle and thread, rules, stitches **Project:** Past Hobbies poster	Informal Letters	**y, igh** by, fly, my, sky, try fight, high, light, night, right	...talk about people's hobbies. ...make comparisons. ...talk about hobbies in the past. ...write an informal letter.
Science: Body movement contract, joints, nerves, organs, relax, system **Project:** Amazing Body poster	Reviews	**ew, ey, e_e** dew, few, new, stew grey, hey, prey, they eve, gene, these	...talk about things people know how to do. ...give opinions. ...describe how my body moves. ...write a review.

Unit 1 Kids in My Class

1:02

1 **Listen, look and say.**

Class Yearbook

1

Trish is **tall** and has got **long light** brown hair. She plays the flute.

2

Darren is **short**. He has got **straight** black hair and glasses. He's **shy**.

3

Sylvia has got brown hair. She carries a **bright** pink backpack.

4

Natalie has got **wavy blonde** hair. She's **clever** and likes to read.

5

Brian has got **dark** brown hair and **glasses**. He's **serious**.

6

Larry has got **light** brown hair. He's **friendly** and very **funny**.

1:03

2 **Listen, find and say.**

3 **Play a game.**

1:04 1:05

4 Listen, look and sing. Which girl is Marie?

Who's That Girl?

It's the first day of school.
We're back in our classes.
Everybody looks different
And I've got new glasses!

Who's that girl
Standing over there?
She's taller than me.
She's got curly dark hair.

In my class are the same friends I know.
But we all change. We all grow. (x2)

It's the first day of school
And I'm back in my chair.
Everybody looks different.
Now I've got straight hair.

Who's that girl?
Oh, wait, that's Marie!
Last time I saw her,
She was shorter than me!

Chorus

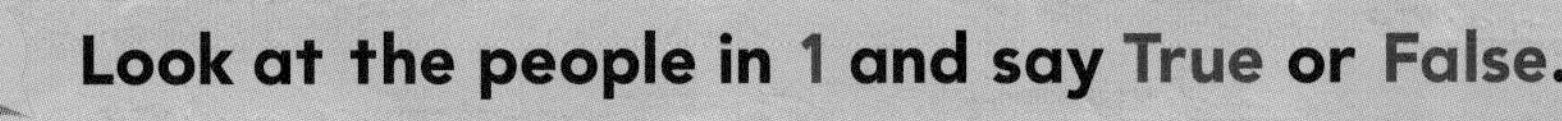

5 Look at the people in 1 and say True or False.

1 Sylvia has got brown hair.
2 Natalie wears glasses.
3 Larry is shy.
4 Brian is serious.
5 Trish plays the saxophone.
6 Darren is tall.

6 Ask and answer about people in your class.

She's tall and has got long black hair. Who is she?

It's Sarah.

THINK BIG Do people in the same family always look the same? Do they sometimes look different?

Listen and read. Who's taller? Amanda or Christina?

1 Christina tells her dad about the new girl at school.

2 Christina and the new girl have got some things in common.

3 But Christina and Amanda are different in some ways, too.

4 Amanda is shorter than Christina.

5 Christina likes her new classmate.

6 Christina is definitely not shy!

8 **Copy the chart. Then read and ✓ or ✗.**

	Christina...	Amanda...
1 has got curly dark hair.		
2 has got long hair.		
3 is tall.		
4 is nice and clever.		
5 is shy.		

THINK BIG **Think of a friend. Explain how you are the same and how you are different.**

9 Listen and look at the sentences. Help Sam and Christina make more.

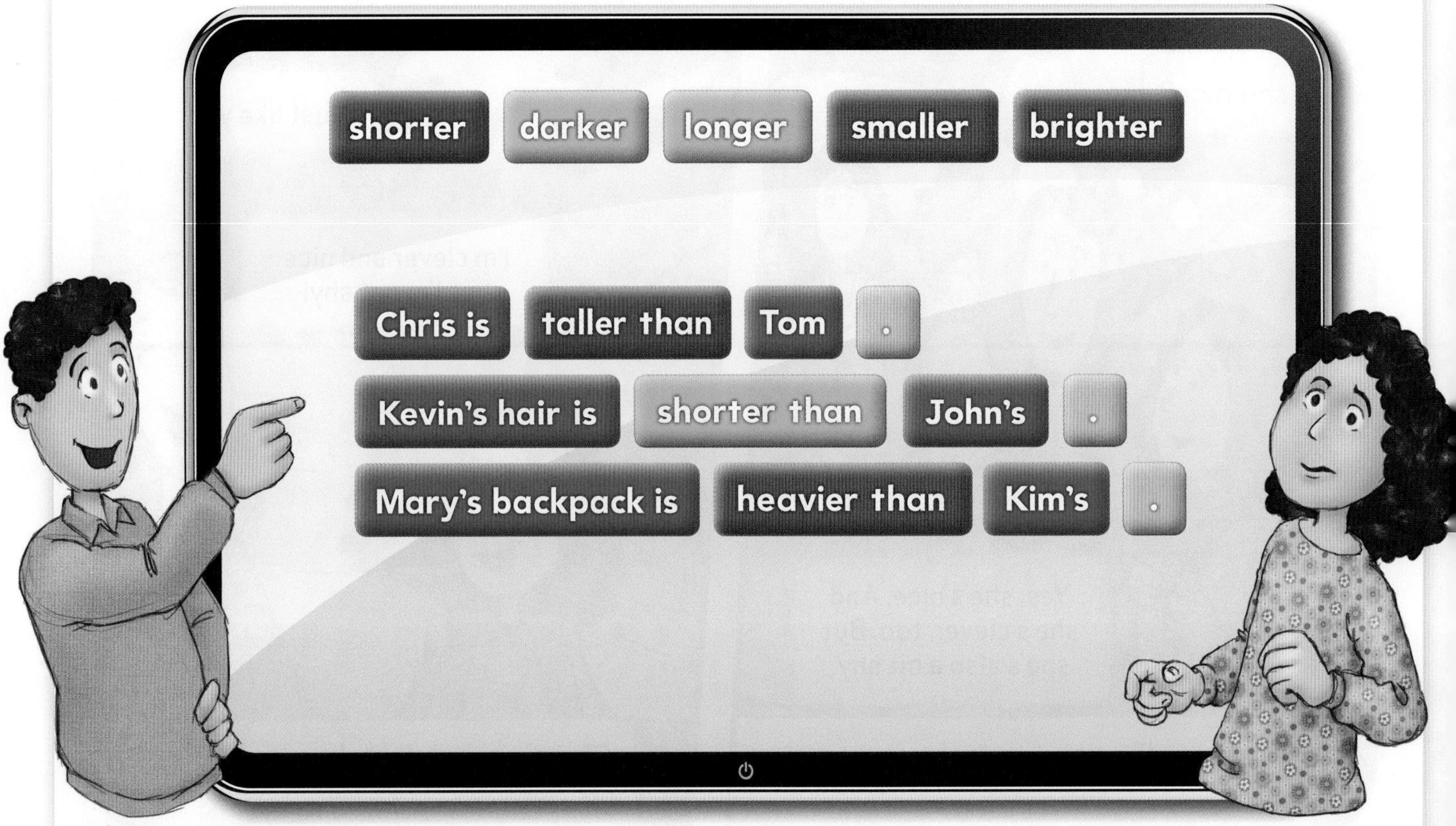

shorter | darker | longer | smaller | brighter

Chris is | taller than | Tom | .

Kevin's hair is | shorter than | John's | .

Mary's backpack is | heavier than | Kim's | .

10 Copy the chart. Then complete.

+er		y +ier		double consonant + er	
1 ?	straighter	curly	3 ?	5 ?	bigger
light	2 ?	4 ?	wavier	red	6 ?

11 Look at the picture. Make sentences using than.

heavy light long short tall

1 Juan is ? Mia.

2 Mia is ? Juan.

3 Mia's hair is ? Juan's.

4 Juan's hair is ? Mia's.

5 Juan's backpack is ? Mia's.

12 Read. Then complete the sentences.

I	my	mine	she	her	hers
you	your	yours	we	our	ours
he	his	his	they	their	theirs

My sister's hair is longer than my hair.	My sister's hair is longer than mine.
My brother's hair is curlier than your hair.	My brother's hair is curlier than [1] ? .
My hair is straighter than his hair.	My hair is straighter than [2] ? .
Our class is bigger than their class.	Our class is bigger than [3] ? .

13 Make new sentences.

hers mine ours yours

1 My sister is younger than **your sister**.

2 His book is heavier than **her book**.

3 Annette's hair is shorter than **my hair**.

4 Their car is bigger than **our car**.

14 Make sentences.

1 my sister/tall/yours
2 his backpack/heavy/mine
3 Annette's legs/long/his
4 my eyes/dark/hers
5 their house/small/ours

15 Describe things in your class with a partner.

Lisa's glasses are darker than Kim's.

Shaun's backpack is brighter than John's.

1:10

16 **Look, listen and repeat.**

birth common fraternal identical quadruplets rare triplets twins

1:11

17 **Listen and read. What's more common? Twins or triplets?**

Twins, Triplets and Quadruplets

identical twins

What are twins, triplets and quadruplets?

Sometimes, a mother has more than one baby at a time. We've got special names for these kinds of babies. When a mother has two babies, we call them 'twins'. 'Triplets' means three babies and 'quadruplets' means four babies!

How common are they?

Twins are the most common. 1 out of every 32 births is a pair of twins. Triplets are more common than quadruplets – about 1 out of every 625 births are triplets but only 1 out of every 9,000 births are quadruplets.

Sometimes, a mother can have five or even six babies at a time but this is even less common.

triplets

Identical or fraternal?

Some twins are 'identical' – they look the same. Other twins are 'fraternal' – they look different.

70% of twins are fraternal twins and 30% are identical twins. So, fraternal twins are more common than identical twins. Identical triplets and quadruplets are very rare. For example, only 8% of triplets are identical and 92% are fraternal. More than 99% of quadruplets are fraternal and less than 1% are identical.

THINK BIG **Do you know any identical or fraternal twins? How would life be different if you were one of a set of quadruplets?**

fraternal twins

quadruplets

18 Copy the chart. Read 17 again and complete.

Number of babies	Name	Number of births	% identical	% fraternal
2	1 ?	1 out of 32	2 ?	70%
3	3 ?	4 ?	8%	5 ?
6 ?	quadruplets	1 out of 9,000	Less than 1%	7 ?

19 Look at 18. Talk with a partner.

less common   more common   quadruplets   triplets   twins

Twins are more common than triplets.

Identical twins are less common than fraternal twins.

PROJECT

20 Make a Famous Twins poster. Then present it to the class.

Famous twins!

John and Edward are brothers. They are singers and TV presenters. They are called Jedward – John + Edward. They are identical twins from Ireland.

1:12

21 **Listen and read. How many different categories are there in the competition?**

The World Beard and Moustache Championship

1

2

3

4

In the 1990s, a group of men in Germany started a competition. They compared their beards and moustaches. Soon competitors came from other countries such as Switzerland, Norway and the United States. They held the World Beard and Moustache Championship every two years. The contest has got eighteen different categories, or types, of beards and moustaches.

The English Moustache is long and goes out to the sides. The Dalí Moustache, named after Spanish painter Salvador Dalí, is long and points up.

The Verdi category gets its name from Italian composer Giuseppe Verdi. This style has got a straight beard and a curly moustache. The Freestyle Beard is really fun. Competitors in this category have got beards of all different shapes and styles.

22 **Look, read and match.**

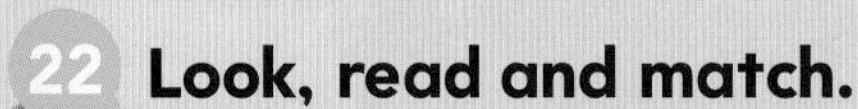

THINK BIG Do you know any famous people with strange hair, moustaches or beards? Why do you think people like doing strange things?

23 Read. Then find the title, topic sentence, detail sentences and final sentence.

A title says what you are going to read about.

A topic sentence gives the main idea of a paragraph.

Detail sentences give us more information.

A final sentence talks about the subject in a different way.

My Best Friend

My best friend's name is Karen.

She's taller than me and her hair is longer than mine. Karen is clever and she is funny, too. We like playing computer games at the weekend.

I'm happy to have a friend like Karen.

24 Read the sentences and say title, topic sentence, detail sentence or final sentence.

1 She is very nice and a lot of fun.
2 I'm always happy to see Aunt Elsie.
3 She likes making biscuits with my sister and me.
4 My favourite aunt is Aunt Elsie.
5 My Aunt Elsie
6 She also likes playing games with us.

25 Look at 24. Order the sentences to make a paragraph.

Writing Steps

26 Write about a friend or relative.

1 Think of a friend or relative.
2 Make a list of what they are like and why you like him/her.
3 Write a title.
4 Write a topic sentence.
5 Write three detail sentences.
6 Write a final sentence.

1:13 27 **Listen, read and repeat.**

1 ear

2 air

1:14 28 **Listen and find. Then say.**

hear

chair

1:15 29 **Listen and blend the sounds.**

1	f-ear	fear	**2**	y-ear	year
3	h-air	hair	**4**	p-air	pair
5	f-air	fair	**6**	d-ear	dear
7	n-ear	near	**8**	s-t-air-s	stairs

1:16 30 **Read aloud. Then listen and chant.**

A boy with big ears and fair hair,
Hears the twins on the stairs.
A boy with big ears and fair hair,
Hears the twins sit on their chairs.

31 **Complete the dialogue.**

blonde clever darker different funny glasses him shy taller yours

A: Is that your brother?

B: Yes, that's Max. We're not the same, we're very 1? . He wears 2? and he's shy.

A: You're not 3? .

B: No! And I'm 4? than 5? .

A: But his hair is 6? than 7? .

B: Yes. I've got 8? hair. His is brown.

A: Is he 9? ?

B: Yes, he's very clever. But I'm 10? !

32 **Make cards with the words below. Then play a game.**

big bright curly dark heavy light long short small tall

I Can

- **make comparisons.**
- **describe people.**
- **talk about twins, triplets and quadruplets.**
- **write a paragraph.**

Unit 2 Our Schedule

1:18

1 Listen, look and say.

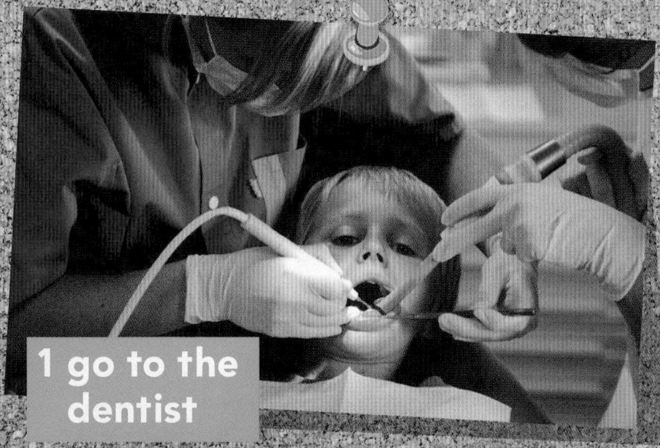

1 go to the dentist

2 go on holiday

3 go to a wedding

4 visit my grandparents

5 eat out

6 have a guitar lesson

1:19

2 Listen, find and say.

3 Play a game.

Listen and sing. Find the nine activities Sam does.

Things We Do!

There are lots and lots of things
That I do every day,
Like go to school, watch a film,
Stay up late and play!

But there are lots of other things
I don't want to do so much,
Like go to the dentist, do the dishes,
Make my bed and such.

How often do you do these things?
Every day? Once a week? Once a year?

I take out the rubbish
On Tuesdays before school.
And I feed our funny cat
But I don't mind – she's cool.

Chorus

Listen and complete.

1 I ? dentist twice a year.
2 They ? every winter.
3 She ? with her parents every Friday.
4 We ? four times a month.

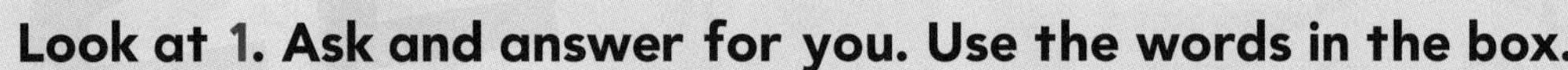

6 **Look at 1. Ask and answer for you. Use the words in the box.**

once * twice ** three times *** every day/week/month/year/summer

How often do you go to the dentist?

I go three times a year.

THINK BIG **What activities should you do once a day? Explain.**

1:24

7 **Listen and read. Where is Christina going this weekend?**

A Lot of Weddings!

1 Christina and Amanda are talking about their weekend plans.

2 Amanda sees her grandma once a week.

3 Christina isn't happy about her weekend plans.

4 Christina doesn't like wearing dresses.

5 Christina has to go to a lot of weddings.

6 Christina is thinking about all the dresses she has to wear to her cousins' weddings.

8 Find the mistakes and correct the sentences.

1 Amanda is going to her friend's house this weekend.
2 Amanda visits her grandma every Sunday.
3 Christina is going to her uncle's wedding.
4 Christina is happy about her weekend.
5 Christina goes to weddings three times a week.
6 Christina likes wearing dresses.

THINK BIG Do you like wearing different clothes for special occasions?
Is it good to have lots of cousins? Why/Why not?

Language in Action

Listen and look at the sentences. Help Sam and Christina make more.

go to a wedding | go to the dentist | eat out

Where | is she | going | tonight | ?

She | 's visiting her grandparents | .

What | are you | doing | after school | ?

I | 'm having a guitar lesson | .

10 Complete the questions. Then match.

1 ? are they doing after school?
2 ? is your sister going?
3 ? are we going after dinner?
4 ? is Mr Lee doing after school?

a She's going to the library.
b They're going shopping.
c He's helping in the school garden.
d We're visiting our grandparents.

11 Put the words in order. Make questions and answers. Then make your own to test your partner.

1 he | tomorrow? | Where | is | going
2 tonight? | are | doing | What | your parents
3 eating out | We're | town. | in
4 going | are | on | My family | holiday | this summer.
5 visiting | He's | his | next | weekend. | friend

12 **Read. Then put these phrases in order. Start with twice a day. Then make sentences for you.**

twice a week ▶ every Thursday ▶ once a month ▶ three times a year ▶ every summer

every month   every spring   every Tuesday
once a day   twice a year   three times a week
twice a day

13 **Answer the questions for you.**

1 How often do you go to the dentist?
2 How often do you play sports?
3 How often does your English teacher give tests?
4 How often does your best friend come to your house?

14 **Correct these sentences for you.**

1 I go to the dentist once a week.
2 My family eat out every weekend.
3 My sister does the dishes twice a year.
4 My grandma makes her bed every winter.
5 I go to a wedding every Saturday.

15 **Ask and answer.**

Look, listen and repeat.

advert attractive believe company popular remember tool

Listen and read. What do companies want you to do?

Advertising

Companies spend a lot of money on advertising. Advertisements, or adverts, are everywhere. They are all around you! Here are some places you can find adverts:

Companies want you to buy things. The job of advertising is to make you want to buy those things. What kinds of tools do advertisers use? They use tools such as these:

Characters: a cartoon character on a box of cereal

Famous People: a basketball player selling sports shoes

Slogans and Jingles: words and tunes that you remember all day

Design: bright colours and interesting images to catch your eye

Many companies try to sell things to kids. Do you believe adverts? Be careful! Advertisers know what you like. They try to make you think that their product can do these things for you:

- make you happier.
- make you more popular.
- make you look more attractive.
- make you look older or younger.

THINK BIG Describe your favourite advert. What tools do the advertisers use? What does the advert tell you?

18 **Read and answer.**

1 Where can you find advertisements?
2 Why do companies advertise their products?
3 What tools do advertisers use to sell their products?
4 What do companies tell you about their products?

19 **Read. Then talk about the advert.**

Do you like this advert?

Yes, and the advert tells you that the cereal will make you healthier.

Yes, I do. It uses a character to sell the product. I like the bear, he's cool!

PROJECT

20 **Make an advert. Then present it to the class.**

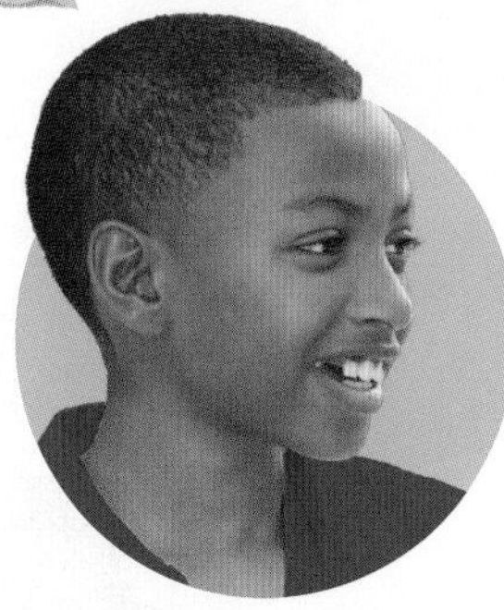

This fantastic bike makes you go faster. It makes you healthier, too. Buy it now! Only €100.

1:29

21 **Listen and read. What does hatman22 do?**

Unusual Habits

People all over the globe have got unusual habits. Here is a page from a website that explores this secret world.

What unusual habits have you got?

birdsong 11:38 a.m. reply

I live in Libya, Africa. It's REALLY hot all the time. So I take a shower three times a day. I know it's a lot. But it cools me off and I like to feel clean!

racerXYZ 11:40 a.m. reply

I've got a strange habit. I never touch doorknobs. I really like sliding doors because they haven't got doorknobs. Lucky for me that I live in Tokyo, Japan. We've got lots of sliding doors here.

snowflake 11:43 a.m. reply

My habits aren't really unusual. Well, there's one. I drink milk twice a day. But always WITH ICE. I can only drink really COLD milk. Our milk here in Hertfordshire, England, is delicious.

hatman22 11:44 a.m. reply

I wear a hat every day. I wear it to school. I wear it to bed. I even wear it in the shower! I guess that's pretty strange. But it's cold where I live – in Rio Grande, Argentina.

ABC_girl 11:49 a.m. reply

You guys haven't got strange habits. Listen to this! I always put the books on my shelf in alphabetical order. I check them every morning. If one is in the wrong place, I fix it.

tbear02 11:57 a.m. reply

I'm a little like you, ABC_girl. I make my bed every morning. Then I put all my stuffed animals on the bed. The animals have to be in the same place every day.

22 **Find these words in the text. What do they mean?**

alphabetical order | doorknobs | ice | sliding doors

THINK BIG **Has anyone in your family got unusual habits? Explain.**

23 **Read and find.**

Sequence words tell the order in which things happen. Here are some examples:

My Day at School

First, we've got a Maths lesson.
Next, we've got a spelling test.
Then we have lunch.
After that, we've got an English lesson.
Finally, we've got a P.E. lesson.

Use first for the first activity. Use finally for the last activity. For the activities in between, you can use the sequence words in any order.

This weekend I'm going to visit my grandparents. First, we're going to the park to fly kites. Next, we're going to the zoo to feed the animals. Then we're going home for lunch. After that, we're playing basketball outside. Finally, we're going to watch a film and eat pizza!

24 **Complete with sequence words.**

My family and I always go to the beach on Saturdays in the summer. [1] ?, we go swimming in the sea. [2] ?, we have a picnic under our big yellow umbrella. [3] ? my mum and dad read magazines and my brothers and I go swimming again all afternoon. [4] ?, we all get in the car to go home. [5] ?, we stop for ice cream!

25 **Write a list of things you do on Saturdays. Then number them in the correct order.**

26 **In your notebook, write a paragraph about what you do on Saturdays. Use sequence words. Share your paragraph with the class.**

Listen, read and repeat.

1 ir

2 ur

Listen and find. Then say.

bird

surf

Listen and blend the sounds.

1	g-ir-l	girl	**2**	sh-ir-t	shirt
3	f-ur	fur	**4**	h-ur-t	hurt
5	s-k-ir-t	skirt	**6**	s-ir	sir
7	c-ur-l	curl	**8**	t-ur-n	turn

Read aloud. Then listen and chant.

Two girls with red curls,
Two cats with black fur,
Two boys with white shirts,
Are watching birds!

31 Look and answer the questions.

1

What are they doing this summer?

2

Where is he going after school?

3

What are you doing this afternoon?

32 Read and choose.

1 How **often/many** do you visit your grandparents?

2 We see them **once/times** a week. We go **on/every** weekend.

3 That's nice. My grandma **always/twice** makes a big pie. It's delicious!

4 Cool. I only see my grandparents **three/three times** a year.

33 Play the Silly Sentences game.

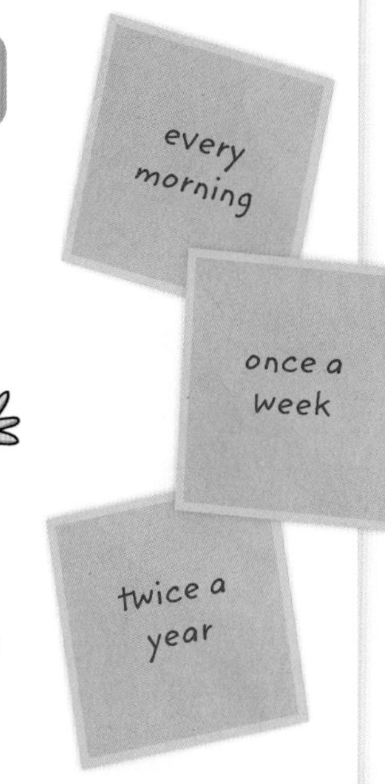

I Can

- talk about what people are doing and where they are going at different times.
- say how often people do things.
- talk about adverts and how they work.

Unit 3 Food Around the World

1:35

1 **Listen, look and say.**

1:36

2 **Listen, find and say.**

3 **Play a game.**

Listen and sing. Find the food.

Would You Like Some?

"Would you like some noodle soup?
Tonight it tastes really nice!"
Sam says, "No, Dad, not right now.
But thanks so much – thanks, anyhow."

Come on, Sam, please have a little taste!
Come on, Sam, don't make a funny face!

"How about a sweet steamed bun?
It's really yummy. Come on, try one!"
Sam says, "No, Dad, not right now
But thanks so much – thanks, anyhow."

"Would you like some chicken curry?"
"No thanks, Dad. I'm in a hurry!"
Sam says, "No, Dad, not right now
But thanks so much – thanks, anyhow."

Chorus

"Come on, Sam. Just one little bite!"
"Oh, really, Dad. Oh, all right!
Mmm. Hey, you're right. It's great!
Please put some more on my plate!"

1:39
5 **Listen and say the food from 1.**

1 
Isabella
Spain

2 
Mei Lin
China

3 
Oliver
Scotland

4 
Ela
Turkey

5 
Alan
United States

THINK BIG **Which child's meals in 5 do you like? Which do you not like? What do you like eating for breakfast and for lunch?**

Listen and read. Does Christina like Sam's cake?

Homemade Lemonade

1 Sam makes some lemonade and cake.

2 Christina would like some cake.

3 Christina doesn't like the cake.

4 Christina would like some lemonade.

5 Christina can't drink the lemonade. It's too sour.

6 Sam realises why Christina doesn't like the lemonade and the cake.

7 **Read and choose. Make correct sentences.**

1 Sam makes some **lemons/lemonade** and cake.
2 Christina **wants/doesn't want** to try some.
3 First, she has **some cake/a lemon** but she doesn't like it.
4 Then she has some lemonade but she **can/can't** drink it.
5 In the lemonade, there's **oranges/lemons**, water and ice.
6 Sam forgot to put in the **salt/sugar**.

THINK BIG **Lemons are sour. Can you think of any other sour foods? Lemonade is sweet. Can you think of any more sweet foods? Which do you prefer? Sour food or sweet food?**

Language in Action

8 Listen and look at the sentences. Help Sam and Christina make more.

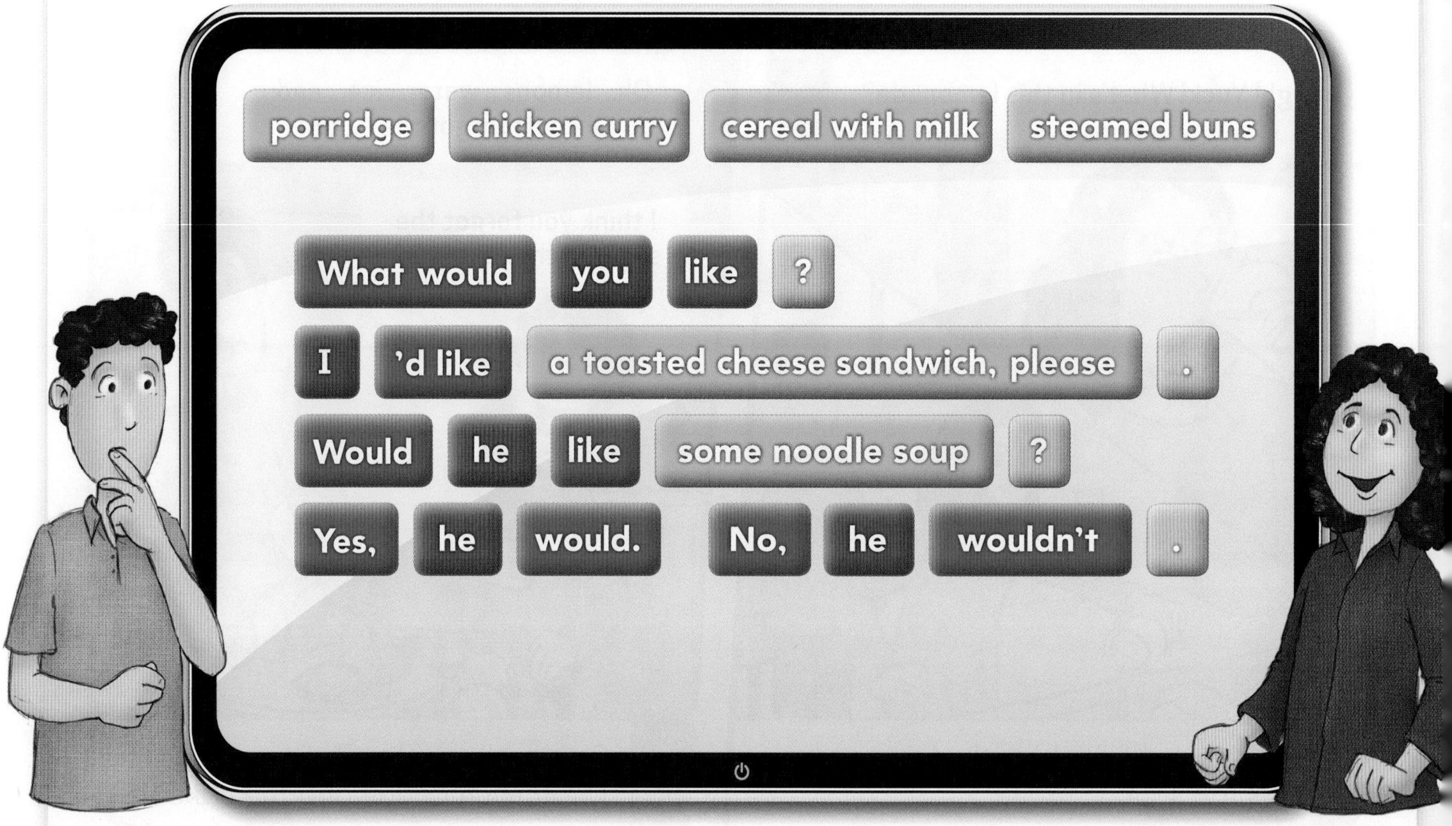

porridge | chicken curry | cereal with milk | steamed buns

What would | you | like | ?

I | 'd like | a toasted cheese sandwich, please | .

Would | he | like | some noodle soup | ?

Yes, | he | would. No, | he | wouldn't | .

9 Look and complete.

1 What ? Jessie ? ?
? some porridge.

2 What ? Jin-Soo ? ?
? some noodle soup.

3 What ? Ms Roberts ? ?
? some watermelon.

4 What ? you ? ?
?

10 **Copy the charts. Then complete with the correct form of do, like or would like.**

Do	you/we/they	1 ?	curry?	Yes,	I/we/they	2 ? .	No,	I/we/they	3 ? .
Does	he/she	4 ?			he/she	5 ? .		he/she	6 ? .

7 ?	you	8 ?	to try some curry?	Yes,	I	9 ? .	No,	I	10 ? .
	he/she				he/she			he/she	
					we			we	
	they				they			they	

11 **Read and complete.**

1 Would your dad like to try a steamed bun? Yes, ? .
2 Would your mum like to try some curry? No, ? .
3 Would you and your friends like to try some lemonade? Yes, ? .
4 Would you like to try some watermelon? ?
5 ? ? Yes, I would.

12 **Put the words in order to make answers. Then match.**

1 What would Helena like for breakfast?
2 What would you like for lunch?
3 What would your uncle like to try?
4 What would they like to eat?
5 Would they like a burger and chips?
6 Would you like to try some paella?

a some cake. | to try | like | He'd
b apple. | She'd | like | an
c would. | Yes, I | Thanks.
d please. | I'd like | noodle soup, | some
e meatballs. | They'd | like | lamb
f wouldn't. | they | No,

1:44

13 **Look, listen and repeat.**

balanced dairy diet grains guide

1:45

14 **Listen and read. What are the five food groups?**

A Healthy Diet

For a balanced diet, you should eat food from each of the five food groups every day: grains, vegetables, fruit, protein and dairy. But how much of each food group should you have?

The chart below is called 'My Plate'. It shows which foods to eat more of and which to eat less of. The Vegetables section is bigger than the Protein section. This means you should eat more vegetables than protein. The Grains section is bigger than the Fruit section, so eat more grains than fruit. The Dairy section is smaller than the others, so eat fewer dairy foods than any other.

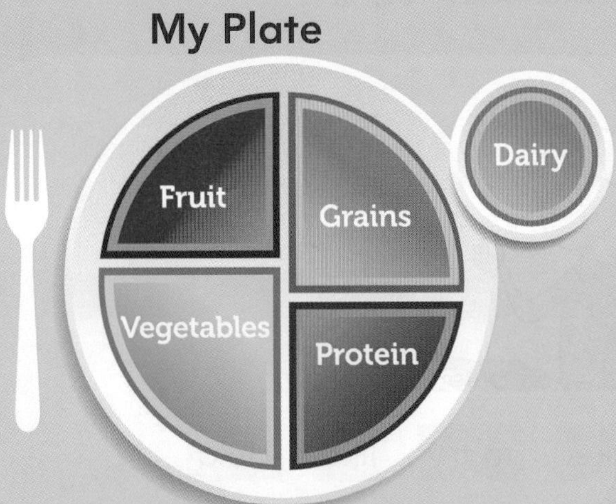

For a healthy body and mind, use the My Plate chart as a guide when you eat and follow these simple rules:

- Eat food you like, but don't eat too much.
- Eat a lot of fruit and vegetables – about half of what you eat should be fruit and vegetables.
- Eat whole grains – half of your grains should be whole grains such as wholemeal bread and pasta.
- Drink fat-free or low-fat milk, not whole milk.
- Stay away from food that is too salty.
- Drink a lot of water – don't choose drinks with a lot of sugar in them.

Can you name two things from each food group? Why is it important to eat a balanced and healthy diet?

15 **Read and say True or False. Correct the sentences that are false.**

1 Eat enough food but not too much.
2 Don't eat too much dairy food.
3 Eat more protein than vegetables.
4 Eat more grains than fruit.
5 Choose a lot of drinks with sugar in them.

16 **Look at the pictures. Talk to your partner about eating a healthy diet.**

fruit

vegetables

grains

dairy

For a healthy body, have a balanced diet.

Don't eat too much salty food.

protein

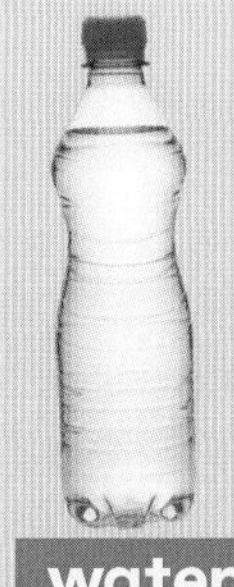

water

salty food

Eat a lot of fruit and vegetables.

PROJECT

17 **Design a Healthy Eating leaflet. Then present it to the class.**

18 **Listen and read. Where is lunch bigger than dinner?**

School Lunches

Every day, kids all over the world eat lunch at school. Some kids bring their lunch from home. But many kids get their lunch from the school canteen. School lunches are different in different parts of the world.

Japan In Japan, kids eat lunch in their classroom. Pupils clear their desks. Then four or five pupils take turns serving the food each day. Rice and soup are often part of school lunches in Japan.

Brazil School lunch in Brazil is usually a meal with a balance of meat or fish, fruit and vegetables and some bread. However, the main part of the meal is almost always rice and beans. Brazilian school lunches are healthy and filling. For most people in Brazil, lunch is bigger than breakfast or dinner.

Zambia In Zambia, many kids eat a dish called *nshima* for lunch. In fact, people in Zambia often eat nshima for both lunch and dinner. Nshima is a sticky dough made from white ground maize. People eat nshima with their hands. They dip it into tasty sauces and usually eat it with some meat or fish.

Italy In Italy, the food in school lunches is often organic, or grown naturally, without chemicals. The food also comes from farms near the school. These lunches usually include pasta or a rice dish called *risotto*. Kids eat salad for lunch, too. Most schools in Italy serve meat only a few times each week.

19 **Read and say the country.**

1 You eat in your classroom.
2 Food comes from farms near the school.
3 You eat with your hands.
4 There is always rice and beans.

Would you like to try any of the food from this unit? Why/Why not?
What is your favourite school lunch? Explain.

1:47

20 Complete the sentences. Use so or because. Then listen and check.

We use so and because to connect sentences.

I like being healthy. I eat yoghurt and fruit for breakfast.
I like being healthy so I eat yoghurt and fruit for breakfast.

I love eating watermelon. It's delicious.
I love eating watermelon because it's delicious.

1 I like eating porridge for breakfast ? it's warm and yummy.
2 I like eating meat ? I often have lamb meatballs.

21 Join the sentences. Use the conjunction.

1 My sister likes chicken curry. She eats it twice a week. (*so*)
2 I usually eat fruit in the morning. It's tasty. (*because*)
3 We can have Mexican food tonight. There's a new restaurant in town. (*because*)
4 I'm going to Spain next month. I'd like to try some paella. (*so*)

22 Find the conjunctions.

I like eating vegetables so I eat them every day. I eat them because they make me feel healthy and are good for my body. I also like drinking fruit juice but I don't really like fruit so I don't eat a lot of fruit. But, I love watermelon! Because I really love it, I sometimes eat it at lunch or dinner!

23 In your notebook, write three sentences about food you like or don't like. Use because and so once.

Phonics | *le, el, al, il*

1:48

24 Listen, read and repeat.

1 le 2 el 3 al 4 il

1:49

25 Listen and find. Then say.

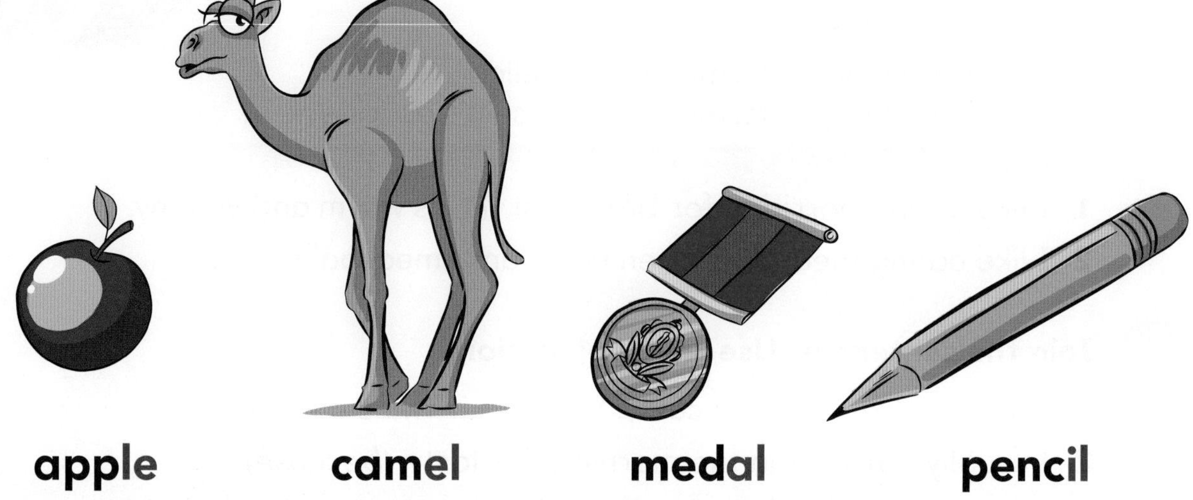

apple **camel** **medal** **pencil**

1:50

26 Listen and blend the sounds.

1	b-u-bb-le	bubble	2	u-n-c-le	uncle
3	t-r-a-v-el	travel	4	a-p-r-il	April
5	s-a-n-d-al-s	sandals	6	t-o-w-el	towel
7	p-u-p-il	pupil	8	l-o-c-al	local

1:51

27 Read aloud. Then listen and chant.

Take your pencil,
Draw a camel,
Draw a medal,
Draw some bubbles.

28 **Complete the dialogue.**

do (x2) like (x3) would (x3)

A: What [1] ? you [2] ? to eat for lunch?

B: I'm not sure.

A: [3] ? you [4] ? to go to the new Thai restaurant?

B: Yes, I [5] ? . What's Thai food like?

A: Some of it is spicy. [6] ? you [7] ? spicy food?

B: Yes, I [8] ? !

A: Great. Let's go.

29 **Make your own restaurant. First, make a menu for breakfast and lunch. Next, take food orders from your classmates. Write the orders.**

Ray's Restaurant

Breakfast		Lunch	
eggs and toast	€3.00	noodle soup	€3.50
yoghurt and fruit	€3.50	chicken curry	€5.25
cereal with milk	€2.75	paella	€4.95
porridge	€2.75	toasted cheese sandwich	€4.50
orange juice	€2.00	burger and chips	€3.75
milk	€1.75	lemonade	€2.00

What would you like for breakfast?

I'd like some porridge, please.

Would you like a drink with that?

Yes, I would. Thank you. I'd like some juice, please.

I Can

- **talk about what people eat.**
- **make polite requests.**
- **talk about a balanced diet.**
- **find and use *because* and *so*.**

How Well Do I Know It? Can I Use It?

1 **Think about it. Read and draw. Practise.**

☺ I know this. I need more practice. I don't know this.

		PAGES			
1	**Appearance:** tall, short, straight black hair, wavy blonde hair...	4			
2	**Personality:** friendly, funny, clever, shy, serious...	4			
3	**Activities:** go to the dentist, go on holiday, go to a wedding, visit my grandparents, eat out, have a guitar lesson...	16			
4	**Expressions of frequency:** every day, once a week, three times a year...	17			
5	**Food:** porridge, noodle soup, lamb meatballs, watermelon...	28			
6	Chris is **taller than** Tom. Mary's backpack is **heavier than** Kim's. My sister's hair is longer than **my hair**. My sister's hair is longer than **mine**.	8–9			
7	**What** are you doing on Friday? We're eating out. **How often** do you have a guitar lesson? I have a guitar lesson once a week.	20–21			
8	What **would** you **like**? **I'd like** some porridge. **Would** she **like to try** some chicken curry? Yes, she **would**./No, she **wouldn't**.	32–33			

I Can Do It!

1:53

2 **Get ready.**

A Complete the dialogue. Then listen and check.

a Ms Hart's hair is shorter than Ms Roberts'.
b She's really nice.
c Ms Hart is bringing pizza to class.
d Ms Hart brought some Indian vegetable curry to class.
e Every Tuesday and Thursday.

Anna: We've got a new Social Science teacher. Her name is Ms Hart.
Dad: What is she like?
Anna: 1 ? . And she's funny, too!
Dad: Oh, I think I saw her. Has she got long blonde hair?
Anna: No, that's Ms Roberts. 2 ? And Ms Hart wears glasses.
Dad: Interesting. When have you got Social Science?
Anna: 3 ? . Right now we're learning about India. 4 ? .
Dad: Really? Was it good?
Anna: Yeah. I loved it! Yesterday we learned about Spain and Ms Hart brought us paella. Today we're learning about Italy. 5 ? .
Dad: Stop. You're making me hungry!

B Practise the dialogue in **A** with a partner.

C Ask and answer the questions with a partner.

1 Would you like to try the food in **A**?
2 What countries do you learn about in Social Science?

1 2 3 4 5 6 7 8 9

Get set.

STEP 1 Create information about someone you would like to have as a pen pal. What is he/she like? Where does he/she live?

STEP 2 Cut out the book outline on page 121 of your Activity Book. Fold it to make a book.

STEP 3 Write about your pen pal in your book. Now you're ready to **GO!**

Go!

A Swap books with three classmates. Write notes about their pen pals in your notebook. Ask and answer questions like the ones below.

- What are the pen pals' names?
- What are they like?/What do they look like?
- What do they like doing?
- What food do they like eating?

_______________'s Pen Pal

Name:

Is like/Looks like:

Likes doing:

Likes eating:

B Tell your class about some of your group's pen pals.

Maria's pen pal lives in China. She likes watching films. She likes eating steamed buns.

5 **Write about yourself in your notebook.**

- Who is taller, you or your best friend?
- What is your best friend like?
- What does your best friend look like?
- What do you like doing after school?
- How often do you play with your friends?
- What food would you like to try?

All About Me

Date: ____________

____

____

1 2 3 4 5 6 7 8 9

How Well Do I Know It Now?

6 A **Look at page 40 and your notebook. Draw again.**

B **Use a different colour.**

C **Read and think.**

I can start the next unit.

I can ask my teacher for help and then start the next unit.

I can practise and then start the next unit.

7 **Rate this Checkpoint.**

very easy | easy | hard | very hard

fun | OK | not fun

Unit 4 How Do You Feel?

Listen, look and say.

1 allergies

2 cough

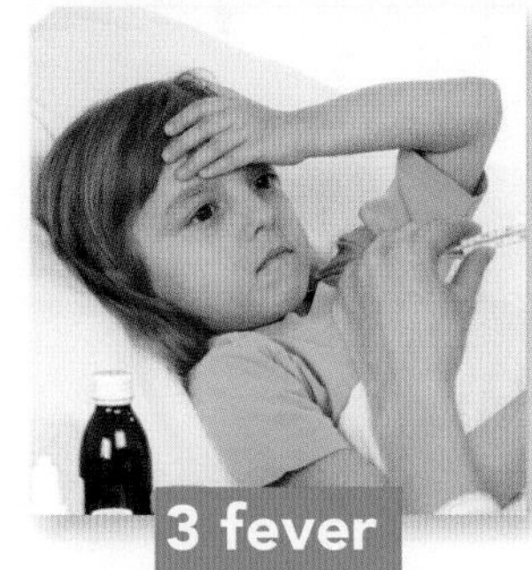
3 fever

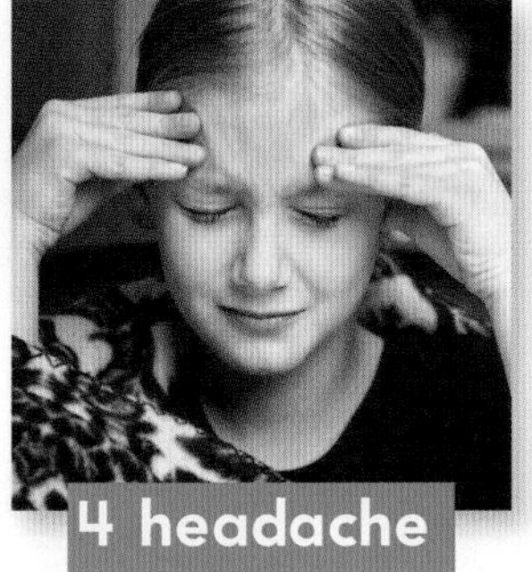
4 headache

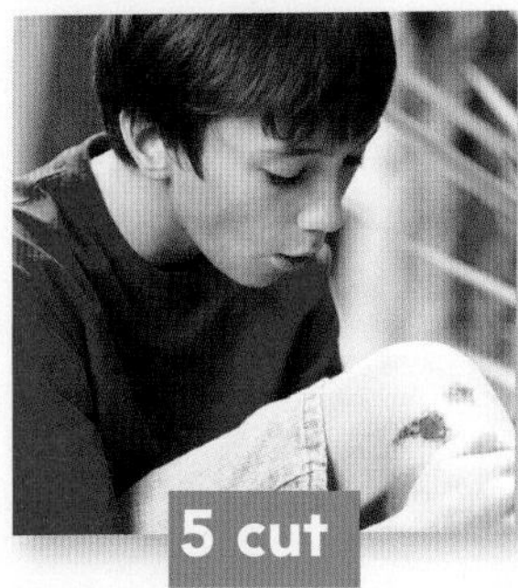
5 cut

6 sneeze

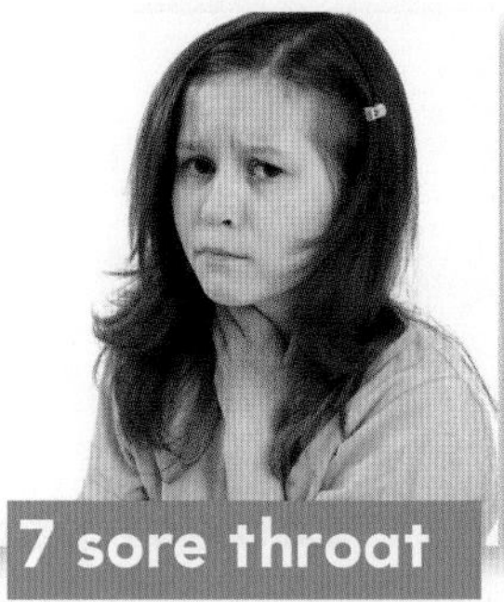
7 sore throat

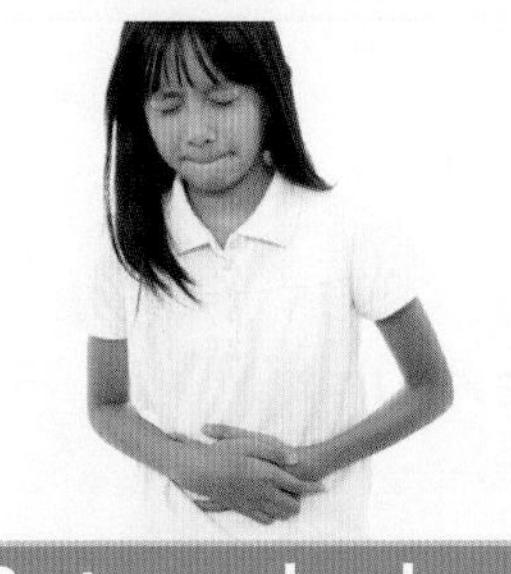
8 stomachache

9 cold

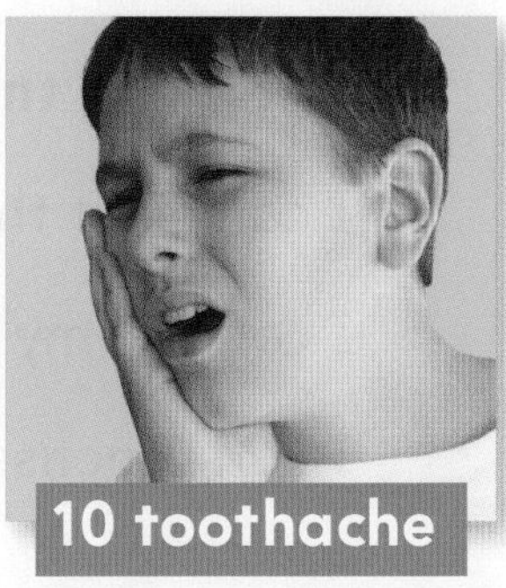
10 toothache

Listen, find and say.

3 **Play a game.**

2:03 2:04

4 **Listen and sing. Who's speaking?**

Stay in Bed and Rest!

You're coughing and
You're sneezing.
You need to stay in bed.
I think you've got a fever.
Here, let me feel your head.
You shouldn't go to
School today.
You should stay
Home instead.

When you're ill or feeling blue,
Your family takes good care
Of you.

You've got a fever and
A cold.
Here's what I suggest:
You should drink some tea
And juice.
Stay in bed and rest!
Listen to your dad, now,
Taking care of yourself
Is best.

Chorus

5 **Choose the correct answer.**

1 Ben has got **bad stomachache/a bad headache**. He ate something bad last night.

2 Philip fell and hurt himself on the playground. He's got a big **fever/cut** on his knee.

3 It's spring and Pablo has got terrible **allergies/cuts**. He's **sore throat/sneezing**.

4 Karen's teeth are sore and she can't eat. She's got a terrible **headache/toothache**.

5 Sandra has got a bad **cold/cut**. She's **allergies/coughing** and she's got a **sore throat/sneezing**. She has to stay home from school.

6 Liz has got a terrible **fever/stomachache** and **headache/cut**. She's very hot and her head is sore.

Read and say what's wrong.

1 The trees are making Sarah sneeze.

2 Emma is bleeding.

Listen and read. Does Christina need a nurse?

You're Hurt!

1 Sam and Christina are eating lunch together at school. Christina's got a problem.

2 Sam gets upset when he sees Christina's arm. He thinks she cut herself.

3 Sam wants to help Christina.

4 Christina doesn't need to go to the nurse. She's OK.

5 Christina cleans her arm.

6 Now Sam doesn't feel very well.

7 **Who says it? Say Sam or Christina.**

1 "You've got a cut."
2 "You should see the school nurse!"
3 "I don't need a nurse."
4 "You should put a plaster on that."
5 "I just need a napkin!"
6 "You shouldn't worry so much!"

THINK BIG **Why did Sam get upset? Why didn't Christina get upset? What should you do if you cut yourself?**

Language in Action

Listen and look at the sentences. Help Sam and Christina make more.

get some rest | put a plaster on it | take some medicine

stay up late | eat so many sweets

You should | stay in bed | .

He should | go to the doctor | .

We shouldn't | go out | .

9 Complete with should or shouldn't.

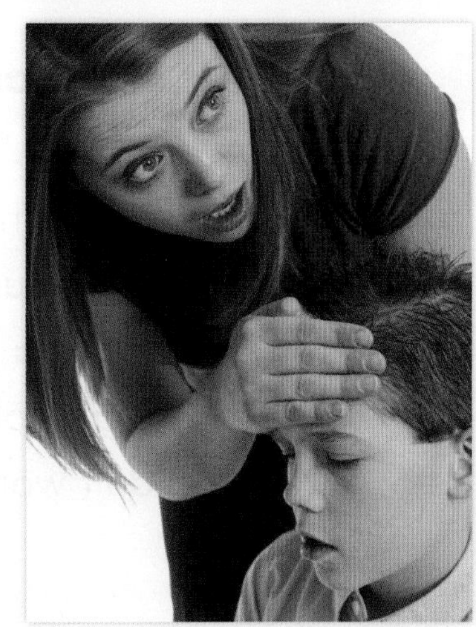

1 **A:** I've got stomachache.
   B: You ? eat so many sweets.

2 **A:** He's got a toothache.
   B: He ? go to the dentist.

3 **A:** They've got colds.
   B: They ? stay in bed and drink a lot of water.

4 **A:** Mary feels ill.
   B: She ? go out and play. She ? go to bed.

10 Role play with a partner.

He's got a cut.

He should go to the nurse.

11 **Read. Then complete the sentences.**

I	myself
you	yourself
he	himself
she	herself
we	ourselves
they	themselves

I should take better care of myself.	My sister should take better care of 1 ? .
We take good care of ourselves.	They take good care of 2 ? .

12 **Complete and match.**

1 My dad eats a healthy breakfast.
2 My sister stays up very late.
3 We always wash our hands.
4 He's got a cut on his arm.

a He should take better care of ? .
b We take good care of ? .
c She should take better care of ? .
d He takes good care of ? .

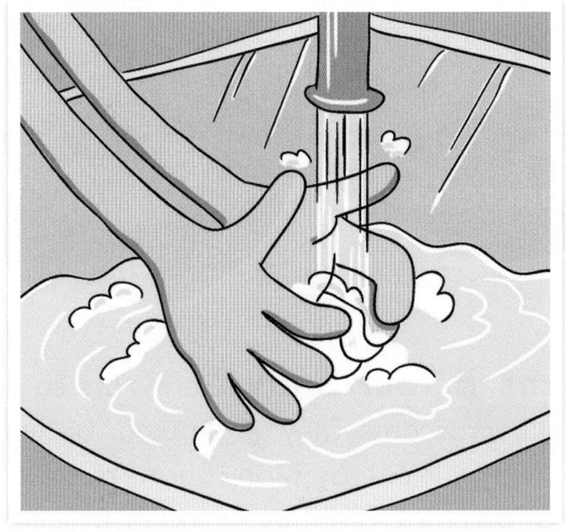

13 **Read and write in your notebook. Use take good care of or should take better care of.**

1 I eat too many sweets.
2 My sister often goes to bed late.
3 My brother exercises every day.
4 My family eat healthy food.
5 You're hurt.
6 My grandparents are 80.

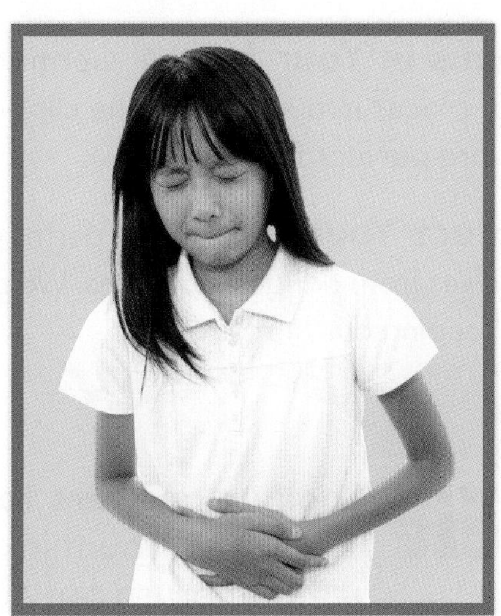

2:09
14 **Look, listen and repeat.**

bacteria enemies fungi germs microscope nutrients poisons protozoa toxins viruses

2:10
15 **Listen and read. What are the four main kinds of germs?**

Germs

Our bodies work hard to stay healthy. But there are many tiny enemies around us that can make us sick. These little enemies are called germs. There are four main kinds of germs: bacteria, viruses, fungi and protozoa.

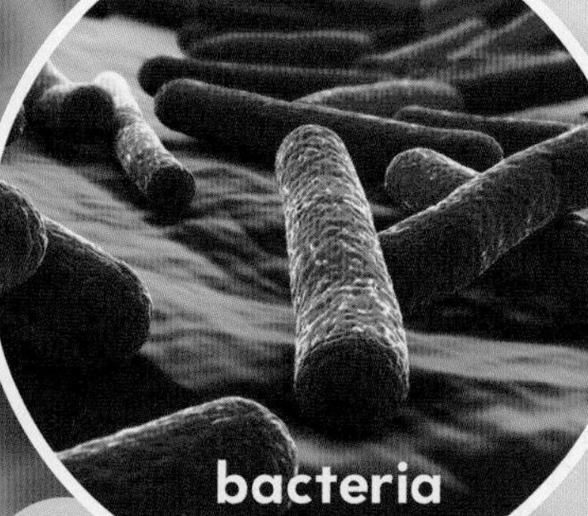

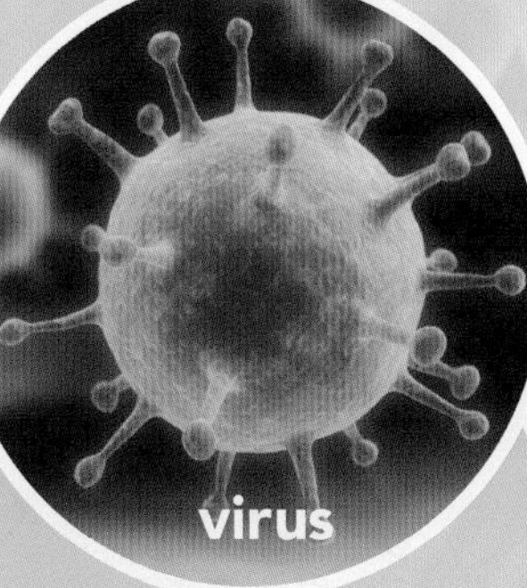

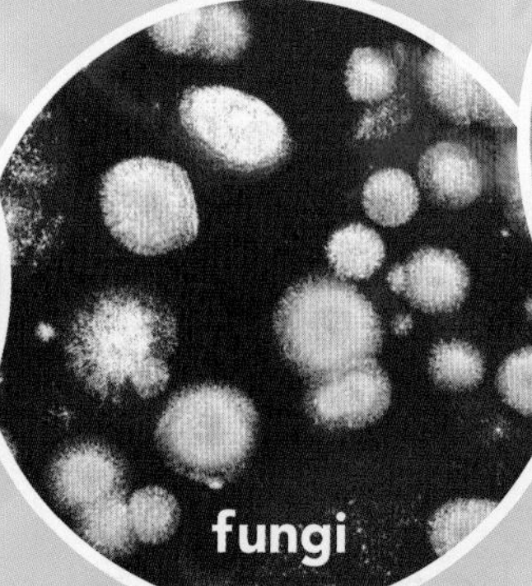

protozoa

Germs in Your Body Germs are so small that we can only see them with a microscope. They get into our bodies, eat up the body's nutrients and take away our energy. Many germs make a kind of poison called a toxin. Toxins can cause fever, coughing or other problems. It is important to stay away from germs as much as possible.

Germs in Your Home Germs are all around us and they get into a lot of places in our homes. The clipboard shows five places in your home that are perfect for germs.

1 the kitchen sink
2 your toothbrush
3 the TV remote control
4 the computer keyboard
5 the bath

Protect Yourself Not all germs are bad. But we should protect ourselves from dangerous germs. We can do this by washing our hands often and keeping our homes clean.

Look up answers to these questions. Discuss with the class.

1 Why do you think the kitchen sink, the bathtub and your toothbrush are easy places for germs to get into?

2 What do you think we should do to protect ourselves from germs in those places?

16 Read and choose the correct answer.

1 Germs get into our bodies and make us...
a ill. b healthy.

2 Bacteria, fungi, viruses and protozoa are all kinds of...
a fever. b germs.

3 We can only see germs through...
a glasses. b a microscope.

4 Germs take away our...
a energy. b food.

5 Germs make a poison called...
a a nutrient. b a toxin.

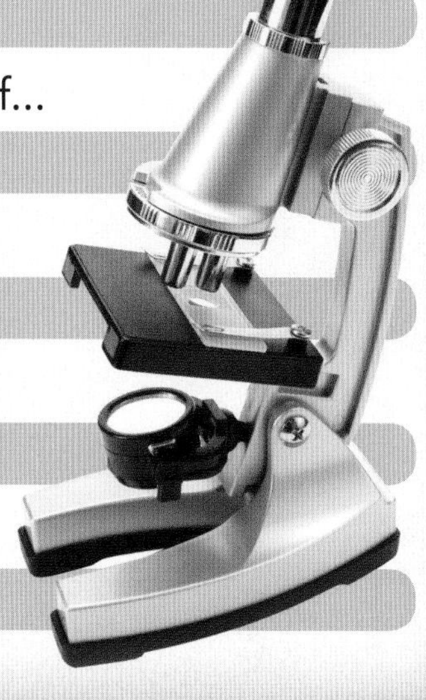

2:11

17 Listen and write True or False in your notebook. Then play with a partner.

Germs take away our energy and make us healthy.

False. They take away our energy and make us ill.

Germs get into our toothbrushes.

True.

PROJECT

18 Make a Protect Yourself checklist. Then present it to the class.

Protect Yourself from Germs

Germs get into a lot of places in our homes and make us ill. Here's what we should do to protect ourselves.

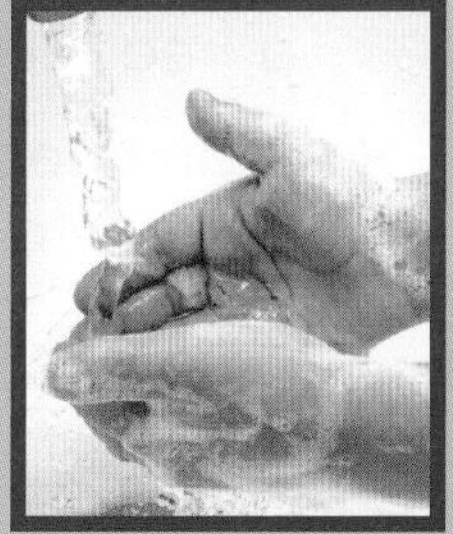

You should wash your hands before eating.

You should cough or sneeze into your arm.

You shouldn't eat or drink with dirty dishes.

2:12

17 **Listen and read. Which remedy do some people use to help with fever?**

Different Remedies

Do you see a doctor every time you've got a cold? Of course not. Your parents just take care of you at home. Maybe they use home remedies. Let's take a look at some popular home remedies used around the world.

Chicken Soup When the first signs of a cold begin, people in many countries make a big pot of hot chicken soup. They eat the soup and rest. Many people believe that chicken soup is a natural and healthy cure for a cold.

Boiled Eggs In China, it is common to rub a hot hard-boiled egg on your face, head and neck to cure a headache. You boil the egg, take off the shell and rub the egg on your head until the egg becomes cool. Many people believe this will help your headache and improve your sleep.

Vinegar People in many countries use vinegar as a medicine. For example, some people in Germany use vinegar to help with sunburn. They rub it onto the skin to make the pain go away. Some people in Russia rub vinegar on the skin to help with a fever.

Tea Many people around the world use tea, especially herbal tea, to cure common problems. Some ingredients in home remedy teas include ginger, garlic, honey and lemon. Popular in Greece, Spain, Korea, Japan and other countries, tea is one of the world's oldest home remedies.

20 **Read and say the remedy.**

1 People in Germany use this on sunburn.

2 You rub this on your head to cure a headache.

3 People around the world drink this to cure common problems.

4 Many people think this is a healthy cure for a cold.

Have you ever tried one of these home remedies? Explain.
Do you think home remedies work? Why/Why not?
What home remedies do people in your family use?

21 Read and choose the sentences where commas are used correctly.

We use a comma (,) between items in a list. We don't use a comma before and or or in a list.

1 I should rest, take medicine and drink tea.
2 I should rest, take medicine, and drink tea.

We use a comma after most sequence words. We don't use a comma after Then.

1 First I brush my teeth. Then, I wash my hands.
2 First, I brush my teeth. Then I wash my hands.

We use a comma before too at the end of a sentence.

1 He should put a plaster on his cut and go to the nurse, too.
2 He should put a plaster on his cut and go to the nurse too.

22 Copy the paragraph in your notebook. Put commas in the correct places.

Here's how I take care of myself and stay healthy. First I exercise every day. I run play football ride my bike and do gymnastics. I like skateboarding too. Next I only eat healthy food. I eat fruit vegetables and yoghurt. I don't eat unhealthy foods like crisps doughnuts or chips. I try to protect myself from germs too. I wash my hands take showers and brush my teeth. Finally I get enough rest and I go to bed early every night.

23 How do you take care of yourself? Write a paragraph in your notebook.

24 2:13 **Listen, read and repeat.**

1 kn

2 wr

25 2:14 **Listen and find. Then say.**

knee

write

26 2:15 **Listen and blend the sounds.**

1	kn-ow	know	**2**	wr-o-ng	wrong
3	wr-a-p	wrap	**4**	kn-o-ck	knock
5	kn-igh-t	knight	**6**	wr-i-s-t	wrist
7	kn-o-t	knot	**8**	wr-e-ck	wreck

27 2:16 **Read aloud. Then listen and chant.**

What's wrong, wrong, wrong?
The knight knocked his
Knee, knee, knee
And his wrist, wrist, wrist.
I know! Wrap his knee
And wrap his wrist!

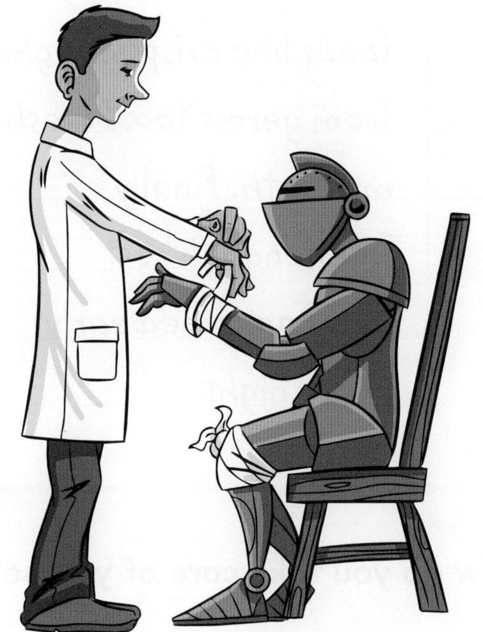

28 Complete the dialogues.

allergies cold cut exercise plaster
should shouldn't stomachache sweets themselves

1 **A:** Oh, no. I've got a ? .
B: You should put a ? on it.

2 **A:** They do ? every day.
B: They take good care of ? .

3 **A:** My sister has got ? .
B: She shouldn't eat so many ? .

4 **A:** His ? are really bad today.
B: He ? take some medicine and stay in the house.

5 **A:** I've got a ? .
B: You ? go to school today.

29 Role play giving advice with a partner.

I Can

- talk about illnesses and health problems.
- give advice.
- talk about different kinds of germs.
- use commas correctly.

Unit 5 Weird and Wild Animals

2:18

1 **Listen, look and say.**

1 Tasmanian devil

Lives in: Australia
Population: between 10,000 and 25,000

2 Andean condor

Lives in: South America
Population: about 10,000

3 angler fish

Lives in: oceans all over the world
Population: we don't know

4 volcano rabbit

Lives on: volcanoes in Mexico
Population: between 2,000 and 12,000

5 coconut crab

Lives on: islands in the Pacific Ocean
Population: more than 100,000

6 tarsier

Lives in: Southeast Asia
Population: we don't know

2:19

2 **Listen, find and say.**

3 **Play a game.**

2:20 2:21

4 **Listen and sing. Why is it important to learn about animals?**

Understanding Animals

Do you know a lot about animals?
How many different kinds there are?
Some are big and some are small
And some are just bizarre!

Understanding animals is good for us to
Do because learning about animals helps
Us and helps them, too!

Some live in trees or in the sea
And some live where it's hot.
Some are beautiful and some are cute
And some are... well, they're not!

Chorus

It's important to learn about animals,
Though many seem strange, it's true.
Because when we learn about animals,
We learn about ourselves, too.

Chorus

5 **Ask and answer about the animals in 1.**

Where do coconut crabs live?

They live on islands in the Pacific Ocean.

How many are there?

There are more than 100,000.

THINK BIG **Find a photo of another weird animal. Tell the class about its population and where it lives.**

2:23

6 **Listen and read. What is the programme about?**

Chimps Are Clever!

1 Christina is watching a TV programme about chimpanzees, or chimps. She's telling Sam about them.

2 Christina explains that chimps make tools to get food.

3 Christina finds out that chimps are endangered.

4 The programme says that there are not many chimps left.

7 Look at the story. Ask and answer.

1 What things can chimps do?
2 How many chimps were there 100 years ago?
3 How many are there now?
4 Why are chimps endangered?
5 Is Sam endangered?

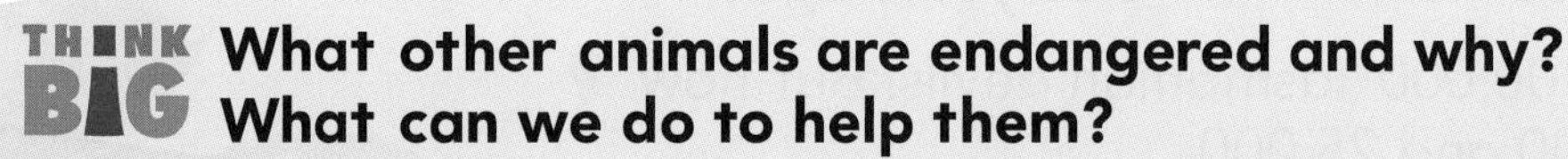

THINK BIG What other animals are endangered and why? What can we do to help them?

Language in Action

2:24

8 **Listen and look at the sentences. Help Sam and Christina make more.**

tigers | 30 years ago

more than 100,000 | fewer than 4,000

black rhinos | 100 years ago

about 100,000 | between 5,000 and 6,000

How many | chimpanzees | were there | 100 years ago | ?

There were | more than one million | .

But now there are | only about 200,000 | .

9 **Complete the sentences.**

1 ? Komodo dragons were there 50 years ago?

? more than 20,000. But now ? probably fewer than 5,000 in the Komodo Islands.

2 ? Andean condors were there in the past?

? many Andean condors in the mountains of South America. But now ? about 10,000.

3 ? Asian elephants were there 100 years ago?

? about 90,000 throughout Asia. But now ? about 45,000.

4 ? Tasmanian devils were there 25 years ago?

? more than 100,000 Tasmanian devils. But now ? between 10,000 and 25,000.

10 **Read. Then complete the sentences.**

Why are Andean flamingos endangered?	They're endangered because their habitat's polluted.
[1] ? are chimpanzees endangered?	They're endangered [2] ? people are destroying their habitat.
[3] ? are tigers endangered?	They're endangered [4] ? people are killing them.

11 **Ask and answer about why each animal is endangered.**

1 why/coconut crabs/endangered
People are eating them./People are destroying their habitat.

2 why/Andean condors/endangered
Other animals are killing them./They're getting ill and dying.

3 why/volcano rabbits/endangered
People are destroying their habitat./There's too much pollution.

4 why/Tasmanian devils/endangered
People are killing them./People are moving into their habitat.

5 why/black rhinos/endangered
People are killing them./People are destroying their habitat.

12 **Work with a partner to find out more about the animals on pages 60 and 61. Discuss.**

Look, listen and repeat.

bamboo burn centimetre (cm) extinct moss pond stream wild

Listen and read. Where do most red pandas live?

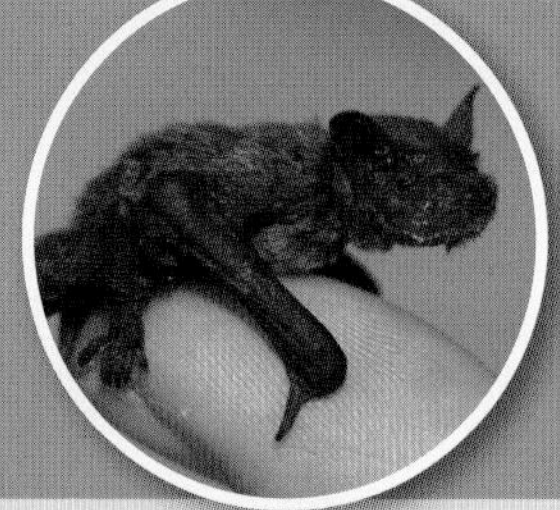

1 This tiny bat is the smallest bat in the world. It is called a **bumblebee bat** because it's the same size as a bumblebee. Most bumblebee bats live in Thailand but some also live in Myanmar. They live in caves in forests. They are endangered because each year farmers burn the forests where they live. Most scientists agree that there are only about 6,000 bumblebee bats left in the wild.

2 This cute animal is the **red panda**. Most red pandas live in mountains in China, Myanmar and Nepal. They live in trees with red moss on their branches. Some scientists believe that the panda's red fur helps it to hide in the moss. Red pandas mainly eat bamboo leaves. Many scientists say that there are fewer than 10,000 red pandas left in the wild.

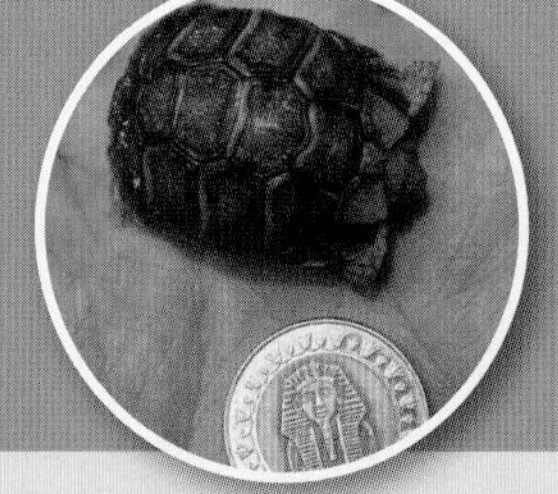

3 The **Egyptian tortoise** is the smallest tortoise in the world. Most Egyptian tortoises are only 10 centimetres when they're fully grown. They live in deserts and their yellow and brown colour helps to camouflage them in the sand. Many tortoises are caught and kept as pets. As a result, some scientists believe there are fewer than 7,500 left in the wild now.

4 This funny looking fish is called the **Mexican walking fish**. It's not really a fish – it's a kind of salamander. It's got legs so it can move around on land. Many of these animals lived in the streams and ponds near Mexico City but most of these ponds are now polluted. Because the walking fish can't live in dirty water, they are almost extinct in the wild.

THINK BIG **Do you know any other cute or interesting animals? Why are they interesting?**

15 **Read and say the animal from 14.**

1 They eat a lot of bamboo leaves.
2 Most are only 10 centimetres long when fully grown.
3 Many of the streams and ponds where they lived are polluted.
4 Most of them live in forest caves in Thailand.
5 Some of them live in mountains in China.
6 Many scientists say they are almost extinct in the wild.

16 **Make sentences with a partner. Then write them in your notebook.**

1
Name: red panda
Habitat: mountains in China, Nepal, Myanmar
Number left in wild: fewer than 10,000
Why endangered: people destroying their habitat

2
Name: Mexican walking fish
Habitat: ponds and streams near Mexico City
Number left in wild: almost extinct
Why endangered: pollution

3
Name: Egyptian tortoise
Habitat: deserts in Egypt
Number left in wild: fewer than 7,500
Why endangered: people catching them as pets

4
Name: bumblebee bat
Habitat: forest caves in Thailand, Myanmar
Number left in wild: about 6,000
Why endangered: farmers burning the forests

Many scientists believe there are only about 6,000 bumblebee bats left in the wild.

Most bumblebee bats live in Thailand.

PROJECT

17 **Make an Endangered Animal fact file. Present it to the class.**

Aye-ayes are endangered because many people believe they're bad luck...

The Aye-Aye

Name: Aye-aye
Habitat: rainforests of Madagascar
Interesting fact: uses a long middle finger to catch insects
Number left in wild: we don't know
Why endangered: people killing them because they think they're bad luck

2:28

18 **Listen and read. What is the only real dragon alive today?**

Dragons

Dragons are mythical creatures. That means they are not real. They are important mythical animals in many cultures around the world. People from North America, South America, Europe, Africa, Oceania and Asia have all got stories about dragons. Antarctica is the only continent in the world with no connection to dragons. But different cultures see dragons differently.

In Asia In Japan, China and Korea, dragons are beautiful and magical creatures. Some stories about them are more than 4,000 years old. Asian dragons haven't got wings. They look like giant lizards. In Asia, dragons are not scary. They are good. They help people.

In the West In Europe, North America and South America, stories about dragons usually show them as evil. Western dragons have got giant wings and they breathe fire. Western dragons are usually scary. However, there are some stories of good dragons in Western culture.

In Australia and Oceania Dragons have got a very long history in Australia and Oceania, too. Some stories of dragons in Oceania are more than 50,000 years old. These dragons are called *bunyip*. The bunyip is a scary monster made of different parts of many animals.

The only real dragon alive today is the Komodo dragon, a very large lizard that lives on a small island in Indonesia. The Komodo dragon is now an endangered species. Many people are trying to help save the world's only living dragon from extinction.

19 **Read and choose Asia, the West or Australia and Oceania.**

1 Dragons here haven't got wings and look like lizards.

2 Dragons here have got big wings and breathe fire.

3 Dragons from this continent help people.

4 Some dragons here are called *bunyip*.

THINK BIG **What stories do you know about dragons? What other mythical creatures do you know?**

20 **Read and choose the correct end mark for each sentence.**

A sentence may end with a full stop (.), a question mark (?) or an exclamation mark (!). These are called end marks.

Use a full stop at the end of a sentence that makes a statement.
I like stories about dragons.

Use a question mark at the end of a question.
Why are tigers endangered?

Use an exclamation mark at the end of a statement which shows a strong feeling.
The Komodo dragon is very scary!

1 How many Tasmanian devils were there in 1920 . / ? / !
2 People are moving into the forest . / ? / !
3 Angler fish are very strange . / ? / !
4 Do you like elephants . / ? / !
5 Mexican walking fish lived in ponds . / ? / !

21 **Rewrite each sentence in your notebook. Use a full stop, a question mark or an exclamation mark.**

1 There are many people that help endangered animals
2 Look at those fantastic dragons
3 Can frogs swim
4 Where do Komodo dragons live
5 Tarsiers are so cute
6 There were more than 100,000 tigers in the 1900s
7 What colour are Andean condors
8 We can do a lot to help endangered animals

22 **Write sentences in your notebook. Write one with a full stop, one with a question mark and one with an exclamation mark.**

2:30 23 **Listen, read and repeat.**

1 ph 2 wh

2:31 24 **Listen and find. Then say.**

phone

whale

2:32 25 **Listen and blend the sounds.**

1	ph-o-t-o	photo	2	ph-a-n-t-o-m	phantom
3	wh-ea-t	wheat	4	d-o-l-ph-i-n	dolphin
5	wh-i-te	white	6	e-l-e-ph-a-n-t	elephant
7	wh-ee-l	wheel	8	wh-e-n	when

2:33 26 **Read aloud. Then listen and chant.**

The phantom's got a photo
On his phone
Of a white wheel
And some wheat.

Complete the sentences with there are or there were.

1 Yesterday, ? three people at the endangered animal meeting. Today, ? eight people at the meeting.

2 ? a million chimpanzees 100 years ago. Now, ? 20,000.

3 ? twelve volcano rabbits on the mountains last week but ? only ten this week.

4 ? a few coconut crabs here last night. Now ? none left.

Ask and answer about these endangered animals.

Name: Asian elephant
100 years ago: 90,000
Now: 45,000
Why endangered: People are killing them.

Name: black rhino
100 years ago: 100,000
Now: between 5,000 and 6,000
Why endangered: People are killing them.

Name: Tasmanian devil
25 years ago: more than 100,000
Now: between 10,000 and 25,000
Why endangered: People are moving into their habitat.

Name: tiger
100 years ago: more than 100,000
Now: fewer than 4,000
Why endangered: People are killing them.

How many tigers were there 100 years ago?

How many are there now?

Why are they endangered?

There were more than 100,000.

There are fewer than 4,000.

Because people are killing them.

I Can

- **talk about different kinds of animals.**
- **say why certain animals are endangered.**
- **use end marks correctly.**

Unit 6 Life Long Ago

2:35

1 **Listen, look and say.**

NOW

1 travel by car

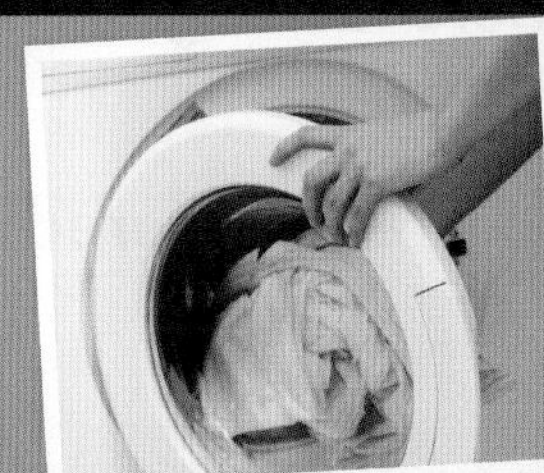
2 wash clothes in a washing machine

3 have a mobile phone

4 have electric lights

5 cook in a microwave

6 listen to an mp3 player

LONG AGO

7 cooked on a coal stove

8 had a phone with an operator

9 travelled by horse and carriage

10 washed clothes by hand

11 had oil lamps

12 listened to the radio

2:36

2 **Listen, find and say.**

3 **Play a game.**

2:37 2:38

4 **Listen and sing. How did people get water one hundred years ago?**

In the Old Days

Life one hundred years ago
Was different, you see.
There were no computers
And there was no TV.

Life was different in the old days.
Life was different in so many ways.

Children used to get water
From pumps or wells outdoors.
Now we just turn on the tap
And out fresh water pours!

Chorus

Life was so much slower!
Few people had a car.
Children used to walk to school
And they walked very far!

Chorus

5 **Choose. Then match the activities of today with activities from the past.**

cook have listen travel wash clothes

1 ? by car
2 ? in a washing machine
3 ? electric lights
4 ? in a microwave
5 ? to an mp3 player

a cooked on a coal stove
b had oil lamps
c listened to the radio
d travelled by horse and carriage
e washed clothes by hand

What else is different now? Tell a partner.

2:40

6 **Listen and read. Did Grandma have a microwave when she was a child?**

Life Was Nicer Then

1 Sam is watching TV and doesn't want to get off the sofa.

2 Grandma doesn't want Sam to be lazy.

3 Most TVs didn't have remote controls when Sam's grandma was a child.

4 Sam's grandma thinks life was a lot nicer when she was young.

5 But now Sam's grandma sometimes uses a microwave to make dinner.

6 Maybe some things about modern life are nicer!

7 **Read and choose.**

When Sam's grandma was a kid...

1 people **watched/didn't watch** TV.

2 people **had/didn't have** remote controls to change channels.

3 people **used/didn't use** to get up to change the channels.

4 life **was/wasn't** simpler and quieter.

5 people **used/didn't use** to cook in a microwave.

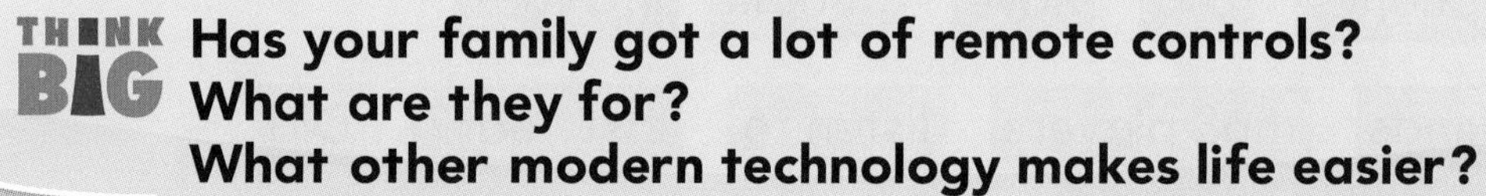

THINK BIG **Has your family got a lot of remote controls?**
What are they for?
What other modern technology makes life easier?

Listen and look at the sentences. Help Sam and Christina make more.

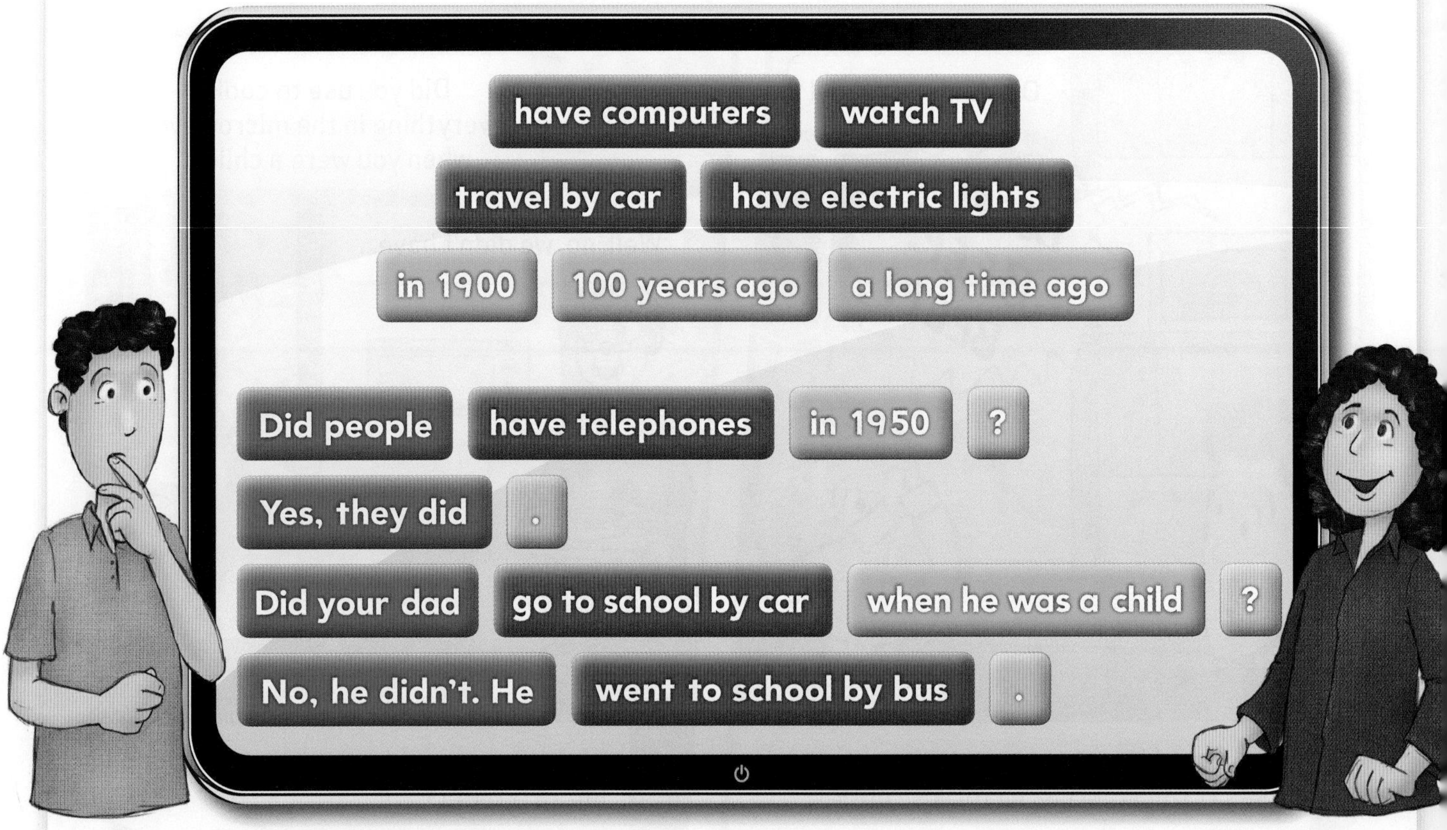

have computers | watch TV
travel by car | have electric lights
in 1900 | 100 years ago | a long time ago

Did people | have telephones | in 1950 | ?
Yes, they did | .
Did your dad | go to school by car | when he was a child | ?
No, he didn't. He | went to school by bus | .

9 Complete the questions and answers.

1 ? your mum ? a car when she was at school?
? . She had a bike.
2 ? people ? video games 20 years ago?
? . There were some very popular video games back then.
3 ? your grandad ? a computer when he was a child?
? . There were no computers then.
4 ? people ? taps in their homes 200 years ago?
? . They got water from a pump outdoors.

10 Write the questions in the right order in your notebook. Then answer.

a mobile phones | Did | have | people | in 1900?
b your friends | mp3 players | listen to | last year? | Did
c your mum | go to school | Did | by horse and carriage?
d wash | Did | people | clothes by hand | a long time ago?

11 **Read. Then choose use to or used to.**

My grandad used to walk to school.	He didn't use to ride a bike.
People [1] ? cook on coal stoves.	They didn't [2] ? cook in microwaves.
Did people use to listen to mp3 players?	No, they didn't. They used to listen to the radio.
Before cars, what did people [3] ? do for transportation?	They [4] ? travel by horse and carriage.
Before computers, how did people [5] ? keep in touch?	They [6] ? write letters.

12 **Make sentences with used to (✔) and didn't use to (✘).**

1 my dad/travel by car/✔
2 my grandma/have a mobile phone/✘
3 people/wash clothes in a washing machine/✘
4 my sister/watch films/✔
5 my brother/play video games/✔
6 people/listen to mp3 players/✘

13 **Read the questions and answer them with your own ideas.**

1 Before taps, how did people use to get water?
2 Before electric lights, what did people use to have?
3 Before TVs, what did people use to do at night?

14 **Ask and answer.**

Did people use to have computers a hundred years ago?

No, they didn't. They used to write letters to keep in touch.

Look, listen and repeat.

average speed   distance travelled   equation   kilometres per hour (km/h)
number of hours   times (x)

2:44
16 **Listen and read. What's the average speed of a modern car?**

How Fast Does it Travel?

1 Horse and Carriage Until the early 1900s, many people travelled by horse and carriage. A horse and carriage had an average speed of 8 kilometres per hour (km/h). If a horse and carriage travels for 4 hours, how far does it travel? Look at the equation:

8 km/h average speed × 4 number of hours = 32 km distance travelled

2 Model T In 1908, the Model T Ford became one of the first popular cars in the world. The average speed of a Model T was about 40 kilometres per hour. If a Model T travels for 4 hours, how far does it travel? Let's do the equation:

40 km/h average speed × 4 number of hours = 160 km distance travelled

3 Modern Car Cars today are much faster than they were in the past. The average speed of a modern car is about 90 kilometres per hour. If a person travels in a modern car for 4 hours, how far does he or she travel? Let's do the equation:

90 km/h average speed × 4 number of hours = 360 km distance travelled

Can you think of ways of travelling that are faster than the modern car? What are the good things and the bad things about travelling fast?

17 **Read. Write the equations and the answers in your notebook.**

1 If a horse and carriage travels for 2 hours, how far does it travel?
2 If a modern car travels for 12 hours, how far does it travel?
3 If a Model T travels for 5 hours, how far does it travel?
4 If the average speed of a person on a bike is 15 km/h, how far does he/she travel in 3 hours?

18 **Make your own equations. Then ask and answer.**

average speed x number of hours = distance travelled →
15 km/h x 2 = 30 km

If the average speed of a bike is 15 kilometres per hour, how far does it travel in 2 hours?

Um... 15 times 2 equals 30. It travels 30 kilometres in 2 hours.

PROJECT

19 **Make a Speed poster. Present it to the class.**

In 1825, the Locomotion 1 travelled at about 25 kilometres per hour...

TRAINS

In 1825, the Locomotion 1 was one of the first passenger steam trains. It travelled at about 25 kilometres per hour.
Now, one of the fastest trains in the world is the French TGV. In 2007, the TGV travelled at 574 kilometres per hour.

2:45

20 **Listen and read. Where do the Koryak people live?**

Traditional Cultures

There are many different groups of people around the world. All these groups have got their own interesting traditions and cultures.

The Maasai

The Maasai people of Kenya, in Africa, are one of the most famous tribes on the planet. The Maasai are *nomadic*. This means they do not live in one place all the time. They move from place to place and make new homes each time they move. They often build their homes in the forests from things they can find in nature – mud, sticks, grass and rocks. Some of their villages haven't got running water or electricity.

The Hmong

The Hmong people of Southeast Asia live in parts of Thailand, Laos and Vietnam. They have got their own language and their own way of life. Many Hmong live the same way now that their ancestors lived 2,000 years ago. You won't find much modern technology in a traditional Hmong village.

The Koryak

The Koryak people live in Russia, on the northern part of the Pacific Coast. The land is Arctic tundra, which is very cold. For food, these people catch fish and herd reindeer. This picture shows Koryak children cooking food for their family. They are wearing warm hats made of reindeer skins.

21 **Find these words in the text. What do they mean?**

ancestors cultures nomadic traditional tundra

THINK BIG **Find out about another traditional culture. How is their life different to yours? How is it the same?**

22 **Read. Then choose the sentences where speech marks are used correctly.**

Speech marks (" ") come in pairs. You put them around the words that people say.

"I had a great time at my grandpa's house," said Jaime.

Commas, full stops, question marks and exclamation marks usually go inside speech marks at the end of what a person says. Commas go outside speech marks if they come before what somebody says.

1 "I used to ride my bike to school, said Maria."

2 "Did they watch TV in the 1930s?" he asked.

3 Miguel yelled, "I got a new mobile phone!"

4 Karen said", I listened to the radio last night".

23 **Read and match. Make sentences.**

1 Tim asked,

2 "My dad used to travel by bus to school,"

3 Claire yelled,

4 Grandpa said,

a "I used to get water from a pump when I was young."

b "How did people use to cook food?"

c Bahar said.

d "I got a new mp3 player yesterday!"

24 **Rewrite the sentences using speech marks in your notebook.**

1 I just saw a movie about Henry Ford and the Model T, he said.

2 What should we do this weekend? she asked.

3 Do your homework before watching TV! his mother told him.

4 Taylor said, I got a new computer.

5 You need to finish your book report by Friday, said Mr Clark.

6 Happy birthday, Grandma Rose! everyone yelled.

25 **Write sentences using speech marks in your notebook.**

2:46

26 **Listen, read and repeat.**

1 ge   2 dge

2:47

27 **Listen and find. Then say.**

page

fridge

2:48

28 **Listen and blend the sounds.**

1	b-a-dge	badge	**2**	e-dge	edge
3	a-ge	age	**4**	s-p-o-n-ge	sponge
5	b-r-i-dge	bridge	**6**	h-e-dge	hedge
7	c-a-ge	cage	**8**	l-ar-ge	large

2:49

29 **Read aloud. Then listen and chant.**

There's a large fridge
On the bridge.
There's a large page
In the cage.

30 **Complete the dialogue.**

carriage did didn't have stoves to use used

A: Life in the old days was hard. They didn't [1] ? to have cars.

B: Really? No cars? How [2] ? they use to travel around?

A: People [3] ? to travel by horse and [4] ? .

B: Wow! Did they [5] ? microwaves back then?

A: No, they [6] ? . People used to cook on coal [7] ? . And they didn't have TVs.

B: No TVs?

A: That's right. People used [8] ? listen to the radio for entertainment.

31 **Work with a partner. Say the differences between the two pictures.**

LONG AGO

A long time ago, people used to wash their clothes by hand.

NOW

Now, many people use washing machines to wash their clothes.

I Can

- talk about the past and the present.
- talk about what people used to do.
- calculate average speed.
- use speech marks correctly.

How Well Do I Know It? Can I Use It?

1 **Think about it. Read and draw. Practise.**

☺ I know this. ☹ I need more practice. ☹ I don't know this.

		PAGES	☺	☹	☹
1	**Health problems:** allergies, cough, cut...	44			
2	**Remedies:** drink some juice, get some rest, take some medicine, see a dentist...	45, 48–49			
3	**Endangered animals:** angler fish, chimpanzee, Komodo dragon, tarsier...	56–61			
4	**Activities (present):** travel by car, have electric lights, cook in a microwave, listen to an mp3 player... **Activities (past):** travelled by horse and carriage, had oil lamps, cooked on a coal stove, listened to the radio...	68–69			
5	You **should** stay in bed. We **shouldn't** stay up late. I should take care better care of **myself**. They take good care of **themselves**.	48–49			
6	**How many** chimpanzees were there 100 years ago? There **were** more than a million. But now there **are** only about 200,000.	60			
7	**Why** are Andean flamingos endangered? They're endangered **because** people are destroying their habitat.	61			
8	**Did** people **have** telephones in 1950? Yes, they **did**. **Did** your dad **listen** to an mp3 player when he was a child? No, he **didn't**. He **listened** to the radio. Before computers, how **did** people **use to** keep in touch? They **used to** write letters.	72–73			

I Can Do It!

2:51

2 Get ready.

A Complete the dialogue. Use the phrases in the box. Then listen and check.

didn't use to watch should go out should watch shouldn't watch used to go out

Mum: What's wrong, Kevin?

Kevin: My eyes are sore.

Mum: I know why. You watch too much TV! You [1] ? and get some exercise.

Kevin: Oh, Mum!

Mum: Listen, I think you [2] ? so much TV. You spend too much time using technology – TV, computer and mobile phone.

Kevin: So... ?

Mum: That's why your eyes are sore. You [3] ? TV for only one hour a day.

Kevin: Only one hour?

Mum: Yes. A long time ago, people [4] ? TV all the time.

Kevin: What did they do?

Mum: Well, they [5] ? and play. So go!

Kevin: Oh, OK, Mum. Maybe you're right.

B Practise the dialogue in **A** with a partner.

C Ask and answer the questions with a partner.

1 What do you think of Kevin's mum's advice?

2 Do you think you should watch less TV? Why/Why not?

3 What should people do to stay healthy?

3 Get set.

STEP 1 Cut out the cards on page 123 of your Activity Book.

STEP 2 Put the cards face down in two piles: green cards and orange cards. Now you're ready to **Go!**

4 Go!

A Read the dialogues.

Dialogue A	Dialogue B
A: What's wrong?	**A:** What's wrong?
B: I've got stomachache.	**B:** I've got stomachache.
A: Why?	**A:** Why?
B: I watched too much TV.	**B:** I ate too many sweets.
A: That doesn't make sense.	**A:** You should go to the school nurse.

B Now play the game. Pick one green card and one orange card. Use them to make a dialogue with a partner. Does the dialogue make sense? If not, pick another orange card. Keep picking orange cards until your dialogue makes sense. Use the card to give advice to your partner. Then change roles and play again.

You should go to the school nurse.

C Act out one of the dialogues for your class.

5 **Write about yourself in your notebook.**

- Do you take care of yourself? Explain.
- What kinds of technology have you got? Did people have this technology 100 years ago? If not, what did they use instead?
- What endangered animals do you know about?
- Why are these animals endangered?
- What can people do to help them?

All About Me Date:____________

How Well Do I Know It Now?

6 A **Look at page 80 and your notebook. Draw again.**

B **Use a different colour.**

C **Read and think.**

I can start the next unit.

I can ask my teacher for help and then start the next unit.

I can practise and then start the next unit.

7 **Rate this Checkpoint.**

☆ very easy ☆ easy ☆ hard ☆ very hard

☆ fun ☆ OK ☆ not fun

Unit 7 Special Days

3:01

1 Listen, look and say.

1 Father's Day

2 my parents' anniversary

3 New Year's Eve/Day

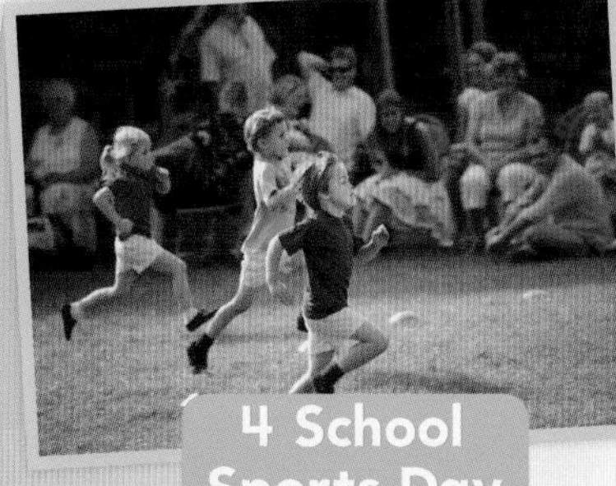

4 School Sports Day

5 Midsummer's Day

6 Earth Day

3:02

2 Listen, find and say.

3 Play a game.

3:03 3:04

4 **Listen and sing. What special day is this Friday?**

What Do We Do on Special Days?

This Friday is a special day –
The last day of the year.
We're going to stay up very late.
At midnight we're going to cheer!

Special days are cool. Special days are fun.
Special days bring special treats for everyone!

On the first of January,
We are going to say,
"Happy New Year!" to everyone
Because it's New Year's Day.

Chorus

There are lots of special days
And this one is a treat.
We're going to have parades and fireworks
And delicious food to eat!

Chorus

3:05

5 **Listen and match the special days to the actions.**

a wear different clothes

b

give/get presents or a card

c

have a party

d

watch a parade

e

watch fireworks

THINK BIG **What other special days can you name?**
What other things do you do on special days?

3:07

6 Listen and read. Why is Sam making a cake?

The Anniversary Party

1 Sam's parents' anniversary is on the 10th.

Oh! That's nice!

Don't worry. I'm going to take care of everything.

2 Sam wants to help his parents celebrate their wedding anniversary.

3 Sam and his family are going to eat out.

4 Sam is planning a little party after the dinner. He's going to give them a card!

7 **Read and say True or False.**

1 In the story, the next day is 10th June.
2 Sam is making a cake for his parents' birthday.
3 They are all going to have dinner at a restaurant.
4 Sam is right about the day but wrong about the month.
5 Sam's parents' anniversary is on 10th June.

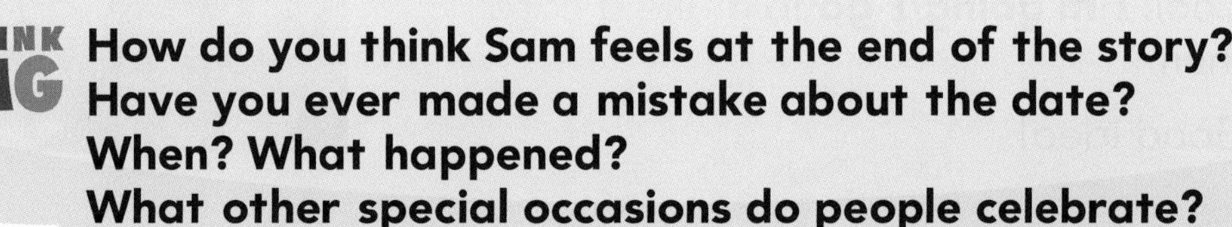

THINK BIG

How do you think Sam feels at the end of the story?
Have you ever made a mistake about the date?
When? What happened?
What other special occasions do people celebrate?

Language in Action

3:08

8 **Listen and look at the sentences. Help Sam and Christina make more.**

9 **Read and complete. Change the words in blue. Then role play with a partner.**

Calvin: When are we **go/going** to go to Grandma's house for their anniversary?

Mum: 10th May.

Calvin: This Saturday? **Are/Is** we going to **have/having** a party?

Mum: Yes. Dad's **going to/going** make some special food and I'm going to bake a cake.

Calvin: Cool. **I'm going/I go** to make a card then.

Mum: Good idea!

10 **Work with a partner. Act out some of the things you do on special days. Ask your partner to guess.**

11 **Read and say. Now look at the calendar and test your partner.**

We write: 1st April

We say: On the first of April

January			
1st first	2nd second	3rd third	4th fourth
5th fifth	6th sixth	7th seventh	8th eighth
9th ninth	10th tenth	11th eleventh	12th twelfth
13th thirteenth	14th fourteenth	15th fifteenth	16th sixteenth
17th seventeenth	18th eighteenth	19th nineteenth	20th twentieth
21st twenty-first	30th thirtieth	31st thirty-first	

12 **Complete the sentences with true answers.**

1 Today is the ? .

2 Tomorrow is the ? .

3 Yesterday was the ? .

4 Next Monday is the ? .

3:10

13 **Listen and choose.**

1 **4th/14th**

2 **12th/20th**

3 **31st/30th**

4 **2nd/20th**

5 **1st/21st**

6 **3rd/4th**

14 **Work with a partner and talk about people you are going to visit.**

Are you going to visit your grandma on the ninth?

No, I'm going to visit my grandma on the tenth.

Content Connection | Geography

3:12
15 **Look, listen and repeat.**

celebrate feast fight glacier guests messy powder

3:13
16 **Listen and read. Which festival is the coldest?**

Unusual Festivals

The world is full of strange and interesting festivals. Here are just a few of the most unusual festivals in the world

Holi – The Festival of Colours

This festival takes place every year in India, Nepal and many other parts of the world in the spring. Holi lasts for many days. During Holi, people throw coloured powder and water at each other. Holi is a festival to celebrate the end of winter and the arrival of spring. It's one of the most colourful festivals in the world.

Tomatina – The Tomato Festival

Every year, on the last Wednesday of August, there is an interesting festival in Buñol, Spain. People come from all over the world for a big food fight. Tomatina is the festival of throwing tomatoes! All over the city, people run through the streets throwing red tomatoes at each other. It's a really messy festival but everyone has a good time.

The Monkey Buffet

On the last weekend in November, the people of Lopburi, Thailand, invite some unusual guests to dinner. Hundreds of monkeys live near the town. Once every year, the monkeys are invited to a feast. The monkeys feast on fruit, nuts and vegetables. People from all over the world come to watch the monkeys eat.

Qoyllurit'i – The Festival of the Snow Star

One of the strangest and coldest festivals on Earth takes place every May or June on a glacier in Peru. Each year many people go to the festival known as Qoyllurit'i. For three days and nights people celebrate with music and dancing on top of the glacier. At the end of the festival, everyone walks out together carrying torches of fire.

THINK BIG **Which of these festivals would you like to see? Why?**

17 **Read and say the name of the festival.**

Festival of the Snow Star   Holi   Monkey Buffet   Tomatina

1 The guests at this festival are monkeys.
2 During this festival, people throw coloured powder at each other.
3 This festival is a messy food fight.
4 This festival celebrates the end of winter.
5 It takes place on the last weekend in November.
6 For three days and nights, people celebrate on top of a glacier.

18 **Talk about the festivals with a partner.**

This festival takes place on the last weekend in November. The guests are monkeys.

It's the Monkey Buffet.

PROJECT

19 **Make an Unusual Festival poster. Then present it to the class.**

Another unusual festival is the cheese rolling festival.

THE CHEESE ROLLING FESTIVAL

The cheese rolling festival takes place in England every June. During the festival, people roll round cheeses down a hill and run after them.

3:14

20 **Listen and read. What are some of the superstitions about leap years?**

Leap Year

How Long Is a Year? Most people say a year is 365 days. It takes about 365 days for Earth to travel around the sun. However, it takes 365 days, 5 hours, 49 minutes and 12 seconds. If a calendar has only got 365 days, what happens to the extra 5 hours, 49 minutes and 12 seconds? The answer is this: Every four years, we add a day to the calendar. It's 29th February and it's called a *leap day*. This kind of year is called a *leap year*. There are 366 days in a leap year.

Leap-Day Superstitions Julius Caesar created leap years in the first century BC. Greeks and Romans were very superstitious about this year. They believed it was unlucky to start a new job, start a journey, marry or buy or sell something. Some people in Greece would still consider it very unlucky to marry on a leap day.

Which Years Are Leap Years? Years that can be divided evenly by four are leap years. The year 2000 was a leap year. Then 2004, 2008 and 2012 were the next leap years. If you know a leaper, make sure you say, "Happy birthday!" Your chance to do that comes only once every four years!

21 **Find the leap years.**

1994

1996

2029

2018

2006

2002

2012

2020

2015

THINK BIG **What other lucky and unlucky superstitions do you know?**

22 Read. Then match the parts of the email.

closing and signature friend's email address greeting
main body of the email your email address
what your email is about

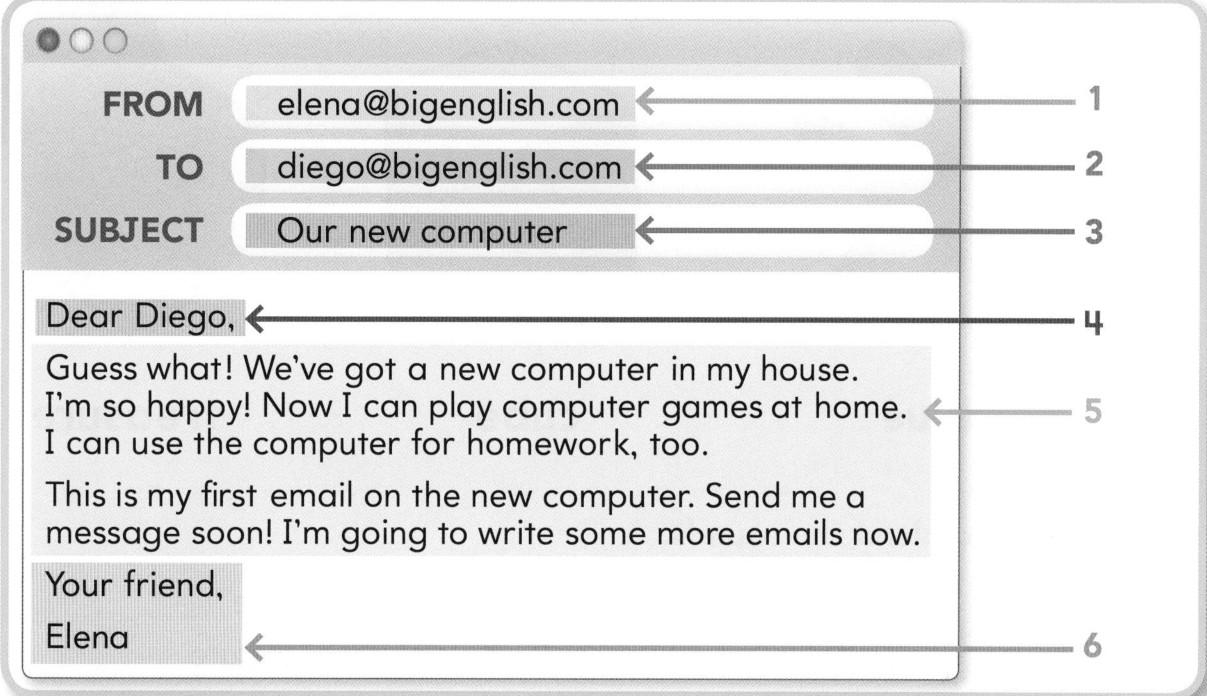

Writing Steps

23 Write an email.

1 Think who you are going to write to.
2 Write the two email addresses.
3 Think about what you are going to write about.
4 Write a subject for your email and your greeting.
5 Think of what you want to write in the email.
6 Write two paragraphs for the body of the email.
7 Write the closing and signature.
8 Read your email and check for mistakes. Now send!

3:15

24 Listen, read and repeat.

1 ue   2 u_e   3 ure

3:16

25 Listen and find. Then say.

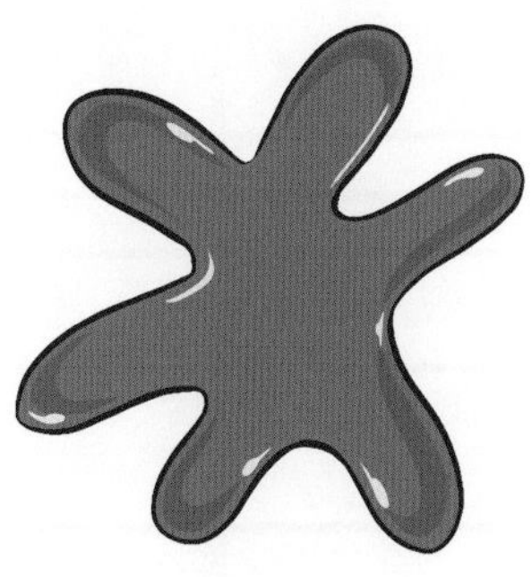

blue **cube** **treasure**

3:17

26 Listen and blend the sounds.

1	g-l-ue	glue	**2**	t-r-ue	true
3	c-u-te	cute	**4**	p-i-c-t-ure	picture
5	n-a-t-ure	nature	**6**	d-u-ke	duke
7	h-u-ge	huge	**8**	S-ue	Sue

3:18

27 Read aloud. Then listen and chant.

Hi, Sue
Is it true?
It's so cute, it's so blue,
It's really huge!
Is that a monster
In the picture?

28 Complete the dialogue.

am	are (x2)	
going	is	on
the	to	

Mum: It's Father's Day this month.
Mike: Is it [1] ? the twenty-seventh?
Mum: No, it's on [2] ? twenty-second.
Mike: What [3] ? we going to do for him?
Mum: We're [4] ? to have a little party.
Mike: [5] ? we going to go out?
Mum: No, we're going [6] ? have the party at home. Aunt Heather [7] ? going to come over and I [8] ? going to make a special dinner for all of us.
Mike: That sounds like fun.

29 Research and answer the questions about a festival in another country.

1 When do people celebrate this day?
2 What do people do on this day?

30 Play the Holiday Plans game.

On New Year's Day, I'm going to watch a parade.

On New Year's Day, Alicia is going to watch a parade and I'm going to sleep until noon.

On New Year's Day, Alicia is going to watch a parade, Robert is going to sleep late and I'm going to visit my grandparents.

I Can

- talk about special days and traditions.
- talk about dates.
- talk about world festivals.
- write an email.

Unit 8 Hobbies

3:20

1 Listen, look and say.

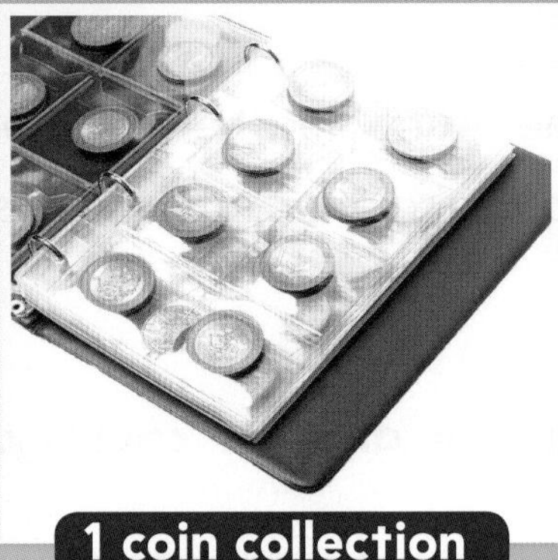
1 coin collection

2 doll collection

3 shell collection

4 toy car collection

5 basketball

6 chess

7 music

8 video games

3:21

2 Listen, find and say.

3 Play a game.

4 Listen and sing. Who is a terrible singer?

The Best and the Worst

Matthew collects toy cars.
He's got one hundred and seven.
But Pam's car collection is bigger.
She's got three hundred
And eleven!

Kay is good at games.
She's really good at chess.
But Paul is even better than Kay.
And Liz, well, she's the best!

What's your hobby, Bobby?
What do you like doing?
What's your hobby, Bobby?
What is fun for you?

Steve is a terrible singer.
Emma's worse than Steve.
But David's singing is the worst.
When he sings, people leave!

It's good to have a hobby.
Some people have got a few.
Even if you're not the best,
It still is fun to do!

Chorus

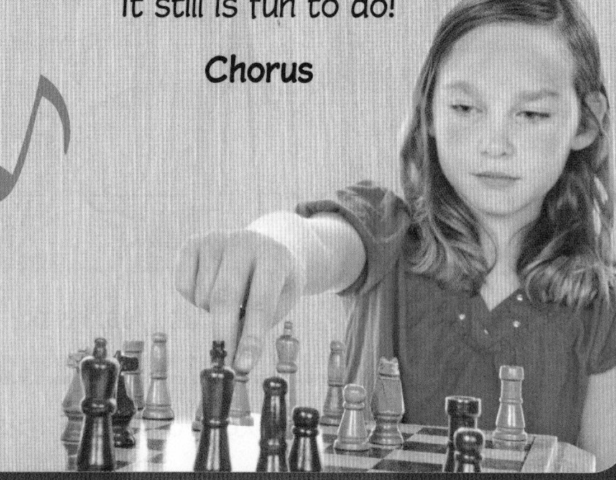

5 Listen and answer. What hobbies do they enjoy?

1 
Freddie

2 
Sylvia

3 
Philip

4 
Kayla

Freddie has got a big toy car collection.

THINK BIG Which child in 5 is the most like you? Why?
What other things can you collect?

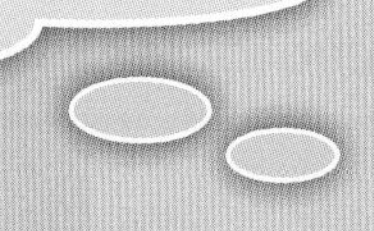

Listen and read. What part is Christina going to have?

The School Play

1 Christina's dad is excited about this year's school play.

2 He wants Christina to be a star.

3 Snow White is the most important character in the play.

4 The Evil Queen is another important character in the play.

7 **Read and say the name: Ruth, Lizzie, Christina or Snow White.**

1 She's the most important character in the play.
2 She's the tallest girl in the class.
3 She's the best actor in the class.
4 She's a better singer than Christina.
5 She's going to be the best tree in the class.

Have you ever acted in a school play? Did you enjoy it? Why/Why not?
Why is Christina's dad proud of her at the end of the story?

Language in Action

3:27

8 **Listen and look at the sentences. Help Sam and Christina make more.**

singer | dancer | basketball player

Laura is a | good | chess player | .

Yoko is a | better | chess player | than | Laura | .

Alex is | the best | chess player | in the class | .

My singing is | bad | .

Her singing is | worse than | mine | .

Claire is | the worst | singer | of all | .

9 **Use the adjectives to complete the sentences.**

1 John's ? artist in our school. (*good*)
2 She's ? girl in our class. (*short*)
3 Julie's ? football player in her team. (*tall*)
4 I've got ? hair in my family. (*long*)
5 My sister's got ? hair in her class. (*curly*)
6 Matt is ? friend I've got. (*funny*)

10 **Think of people in your family. Talk about the things they can do.**

My dad is a good singer. My sister is the best chess player in the family.

11 Read. Then complete the dialogue.

I'm good at video games.
He's good at music.
She's bad at chess.
They're bad at basketball.

A: What are you good [1] ? , Sally?

B: Umm. I love playing the guitar. I think I'm [2] ? at music.

A: You definitely are. What are you [3] ? at?

B: I'm pretty [4] ? basketball but I am OK at football.

12 Look at the pictures. Complete the dialogues.

bad better good than (x2) the best the worst worse

1

A: Sam is a ? singer.

B: Yes. But Mike is ? Sam.

A: Yes. But Terry is ? singer of all. He really can't sing!

2

A: Vincent is a ? actor.

B: Yes. But Tim is ? Vincent.

A: True! But Louisa is ? in our class.

13 Work with a partner and find out more about people in your class. Report your findings to the class.

3:29

14 **Look, listen and repeat.**

croquet employer fabric marbles needle and thread rules stitches

3:30

15 **Listen and read. What hobbies did children have in the 19th century?**

Hobbies in the Past

In the 19th century, there were many popular hobbies. Let's learn about some of these hobbies.

SPORTS

Many sports that we play today were played in the 19th century. Football became popular and the game was given rules for the first time. Many football clubs were started by employers so that the workers could play and could stay fit. Tennis and croquet were also popular and they were played by both men and women.

EMBROIDERY AND SEWING

Many women and girls spent their spare time doing sewing and embroidery. They used a needle and thread to make tiny stitches on a piece of fabric. They created beautiful pictures of flowers, birds and other patterns. They used to embroider cushions, tablecloths and clothes such as gloves.

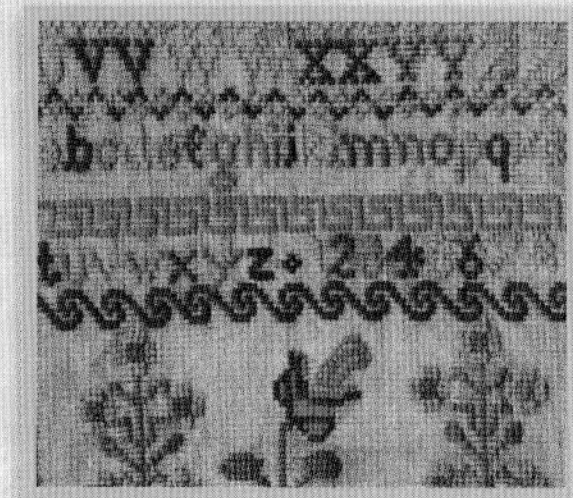

CHILDREN'S HOBBIES

Girls in the 19th century used to play with dolls and doll's houses. The dolls' heads were often made of china and the bodies were made of wood or calico. Rocking horses were also very popular. They were always white and grey and the tails were made of real horsehair. Boys used to play with toy trains and railways.

COLLECTING

People in the 19th century loved nature. One popular hobby was collecting and drawing butterflies. People used to catch butterflies in nets, then they put them on special boards with a pin. They used to draw the butterflies very carefully so they showed all the details and colours.

THINK BIG **Which of these hobbies would you like to do? Can you think of any hobbies people did in the past in your country?**

16 Read and say True or False.

1 Football was given rules for the first time in the 19th century.
2 People didn't use to catch butterflies.
3 Tennis and croquet were played only by men.
4 Dolls were made of plastic in the 19th century.
5 Women and girls used to embroider cushions and tablecloths.
6 The tails of rocking horses were made of real horsehair.

17 Choose a hobby from the past. Talk about it with a partner.

Girls used to play with dolls and doll's houses.

The dolls were made of china and wood.

PROJECT

18 Make a Past Hobbies poster. Then present it to the class.

In the 19th century, children used to have different hobbies.

PAST HOBBIES

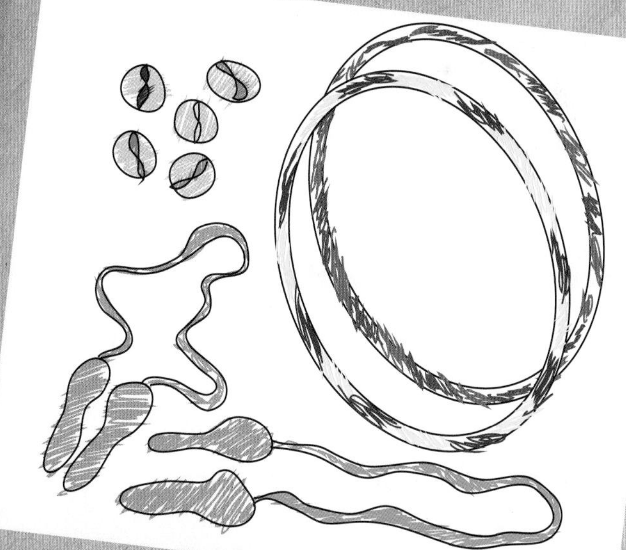

In the 19th century, children used to play with marbles. The marbles were made of glass. They also used to play with hoops and skipping ropes.

3:37

19 **Listen and read. Where can you find these three museums?**

The World's Weirdest Collections

Some museums show us how people used to live a long time ago. But there are other kinds of museums in the world, too. Here are some facts about a few 'weird museums'.

The Hair Museum In Avanos, in Turkey, you can find a hair museum! It all started when a potter from the town was saying goodbye to a friend who was moving away. This friend gave the potter a piece of hair and he put it in his shop. When other people saw the hair, they wanted to leave a piece of hair as well! Now there are thousands of pieces of hair! Each one is labelled with the name of the person and the date it was cut.

The International UFO Museum and Research Centre

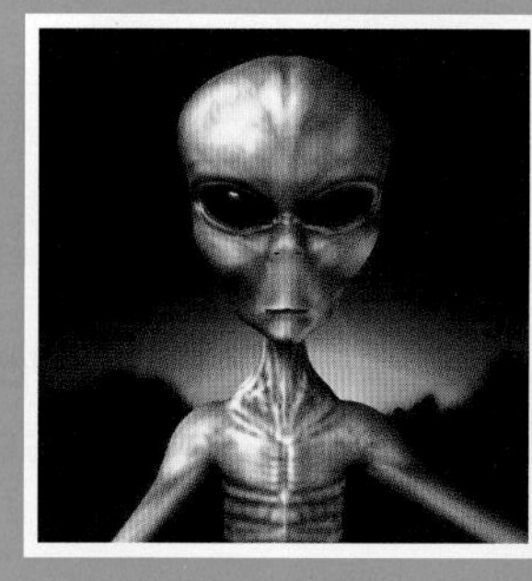

Many people believe that a UFO landed in Roswell, New Mexico, USA, in 1947. If you want to know more about UFOs, you can visit the International UFO Museum and Research Centre. The centre holds a UFO Festival every year at the museum. At the festival, experts from around the world come to talk about the latest news in UFO research.

The Museum of Underwater Art

To visit this museum, you need to swim. In the ocean near Cancún, Mexico, there is a collection of statues. This museum is inside the National Marine Park of the Yucatán Peninsula of Mexico and it displays a large number of sculptures. The British artist, Jason deCaires Taylor, wants the animals and plants in the ocean to become part of the artwork.

20 **Read and answer the questions.**

1 What information can you find out at the Hair Museum?
2 Where can you find statues?
3 What does Jason deCaires Taylor want?
4 How often is there a UFO Festival?

THINK BIG **Which is the strangest collection? Do you know of any other strange collections?**

21 **Read. Then match the parts of the informal letter.**

address   body of informal letter   closing and signature   date   greeting

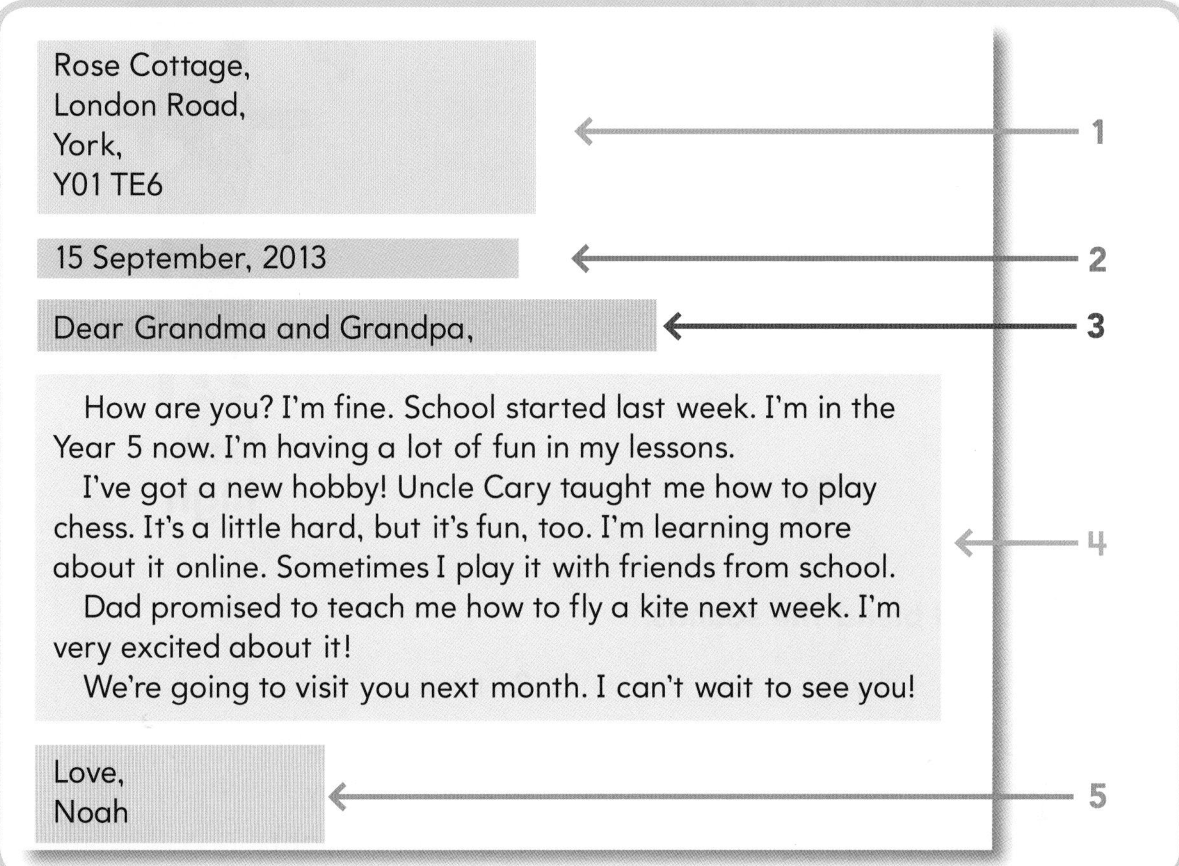

Rose Cottage,
London Road,
York,
Y01 TE6 ← 1

15 September, 2013 ← 2

Dear Grandma and Grandpa, ← 3

How are you? I'm fine. School started last week. I'm in the Year 5 now. I'm having a lot of fun in my lessons.

I've got a new hobby! Uncle Cary taught me how to play chess. It's a little hard, but it's fun, too. I'm learning more about it online. Sometimes I play it with friends from school.

Dad promised to teach me how to fly a kite next week. I'm very excited about it!

We're going to visit you next month. I can't wait to see you! ← 4

Love,
Noah ← 5

Writing Steps

22 **Write an informal letter to a friend or family member.**

1 Write your address.
2 Write the date.
3 Think of a person to write to.
4 Choose a hobby to write about.
5 Think of what you want to tell him/her.
6 Finish with a final sentence.
7 Write a final sentence.
8 Finish with the closing and signature.

23 **Listen, read and repeat.**

1 y

2 igh

24 **Listen and find. Then say.**

fly

high

25 **Listen and blend the sounds.**

1 s-k-y sky

2 t-r-y try

3 m-y my

4 l-igh-t light

5 f-igh-t fight

6 b-y by

7 n-igh-t night

8 r-igh-t right

26 **Read aloud. Then listen and chant.**

Let's fly, let's fight.
Let's try
And light the sky
At night!

27 Complete the sentences.

1 Terrence's shell collection is ? in the class. (*good*)

2 Look at this. This is ? coin in my coin collection. (*old*)

3 The dolls in Sandy's collection are ? than my dolls. (*good*)

4 I've got a lot of small cars in my collection but this one is ? . (*small*)

28 Look and complete the sentences.

1 Mark is a ? dancer than Kelly.

2 Sharon is a ? dancer than Mark.

3 Sharon is ? dancer in the group.

4 Mark is ? dancer of the three students.

29 Complete with information about yourself. Find out about your partner. Then report to the class.

1 I am good at... . ... is a better... than I am.

2 I am not good at... . ... is a worse... .

I Can

- **talk about people's hobbies.**
- **make comparisons.**
- **talk about hobbies in the past.**
- **write an informal letter.**

Unit 9 Learning New Things

3:37

1 Listen, look and say.

3:38

2 Listen, find and say.

3 Play a game.

3:39 3.40

4 **Listen and sing. What's brilliant and cool?**

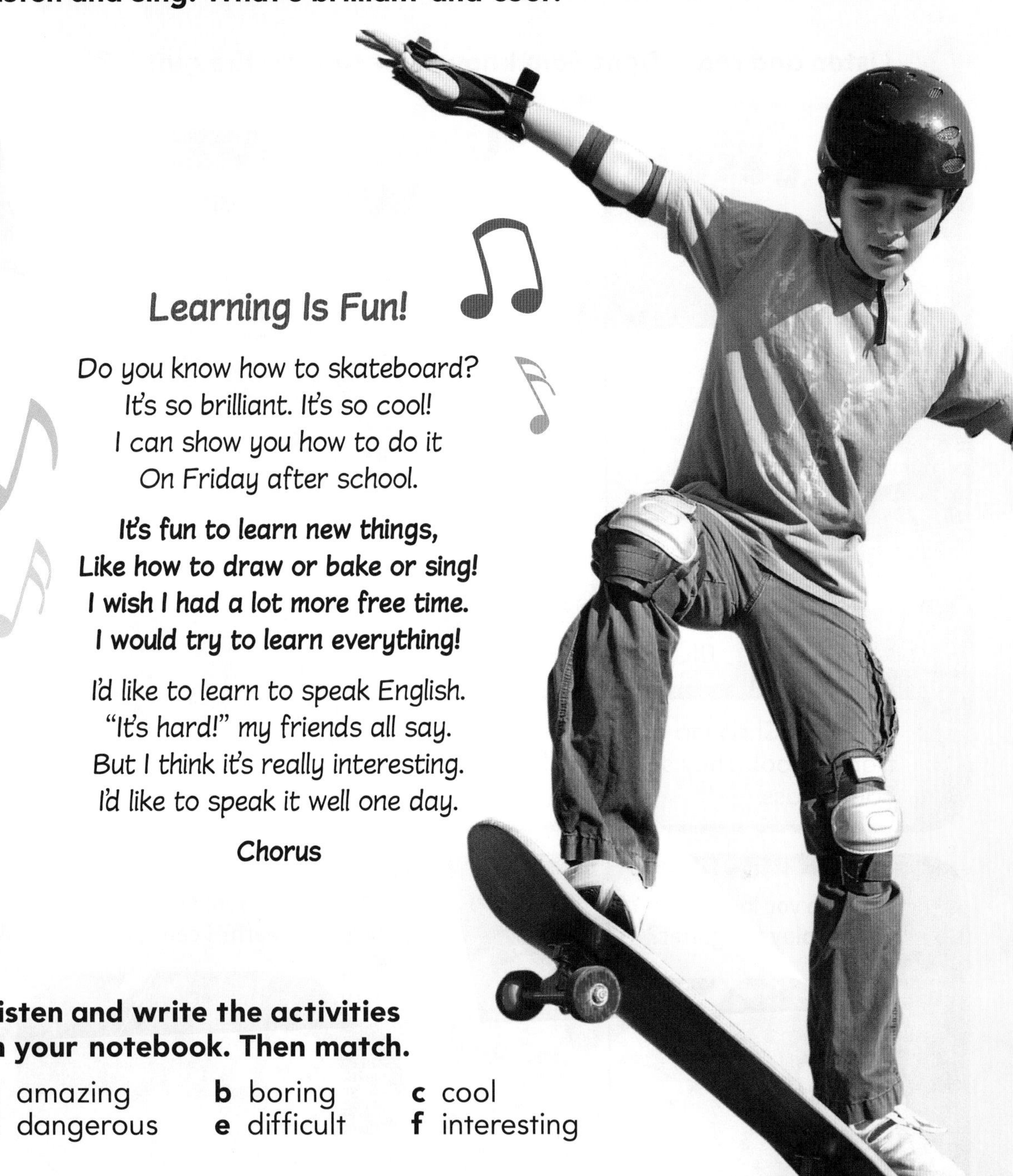

Learning Is Fun!

Do you know how to skateboard?
It's so brilliant. It's so cool!
I can show you how to do it
On Friday after school.

It's fun to learn new things,
Like how to draw or bake or sing!
I wish I had a lot more free time.
I would try to learn everything!

I'd like to learn to speak English.
"It's hard!" my friends all say.
But I think it's really interesting.
I'd like to speak it well one day.

Chorus

3:41

5 **Listen and write the activities in your notebook. Then match.**

a amazing **b** boring **c** cool
d dangerous **e** difficult **f** interesting

THINK BIG **Which things in 1 can you do?**
What do you think of the talents in 1? Use the words from 5 in your answers.
What skills would you like to learn? Why?

Listen and read. Does Sam know how to play the guitar?

The Best in the Class

1 Sam and Christina are walking home from school. They see a boy from Sam's class.

2 Sam thinks that Jake can play the guitar very well.

3 Sam doesn't know how to play the guitar.

4 Jake wants to teach Sam how to play the guitar.

5 Sam tries to play the guitar. But he's not very good!

6 Christina thinks Sam's guitar playing is awful.

7 Correct the sentences. Write the correct sentences in your notebook.

1 Jake is really good at playing the piano.
2 Sam knows how to play the guitar.
3 Sam wants to teach Jake to play the guitar.
4 Sam is good at playing the guitar.
5 Christina thinks Sam's playing is great.

THINK BIG What are you good at doing? What do you have to do to learn how to do a new thing well?

Listen and look at the sentences. Help Sam and Christina make more.

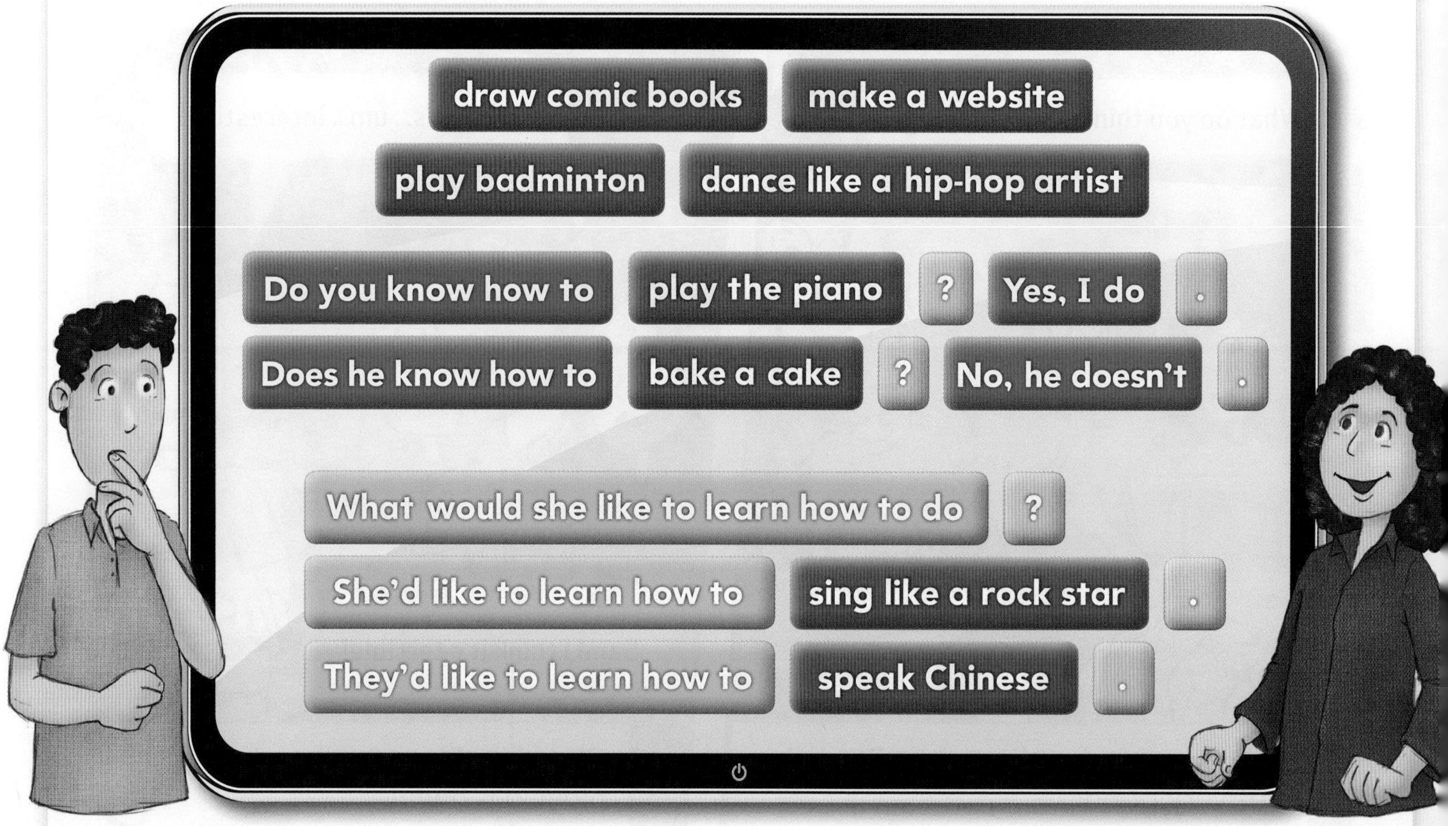

draw comic books | make a website | play badminton | dance like a hip-hop artist

Do you know how to | play the piano | ? | Yes, I do | .

Does he know how to | bake a cake | ? | No, he doesn't | .

What would she like to learn how to do | ?

She'd like to learn how to | sing like a rock star | .

They'd like to learn how to | speak Chinese | .

9 **Complete the questions and answers.**

1 Do you ? the guitar?
? . But I can play the piano.

2 Does he ? dance?
? . He dances every weekend.

3 ? sing?
? . They sing very well.

4 ? draw?
? . She's terrible at art.

10 **Look and read. Write the answers in your notebook.**

1

What would they like to learn how to do?

2

What would she like to learn how to do?

3

What would he like to learn how to do?

11 **Read. Then complete the sentences.**

What do you think of snowboarding?	I think it's dangerous.
What does she think of baking cakes?	She thinks it's boring.
What do they [1] ? of learning Chinese?	They [2] ? it's difficult.
What does he [3] ? of playing the piano?	He [4] ? it's amazing.

12 **Write questions and answers in your notebook.**

1

she/make pizza/?
cool/.

2

he/skateboard/?
fun/.

3

they/build a robot/?
difficult/.

4

you/watch tennis/?
interesting/.

13 **Ask and answer with a partner.**

What do you think of hip-hop dancing?

I think it's amazing.

3:46

14 **Look, listen and repeat.**

contract joints nerves organs relax system

3:47

15 **Listen and read. What three things help us move our bodies?**

Moving Your Body

With every move you make, you are using your bones, muscles and joints. These three kinds of body parts make up your musculoskeletal system. Without your musculoskeletal system, you would not be able to stand, walk or move in any way.

Your bones are your body's frame. They support the organs within your body and give the body shape. Without bones, your body would look like an octopus!

Your joints connect two or more bones to each other. Joints are important because they allow you to be flexible. Without working joints, your body would not be able to move.

Your muscles are also important for motion. Muscles are strong and flexible. They pull the bones in different directions. By pulling your bones in different directions, they help your body to move.

Of course, your muscles, bones and joints do not move by themselves. Your brain and your nerves help out. For example, if you want to kick a football, your brain needs to tell your nerves that you want to move your foot. Your nerves send a message to your muscles. Your muscles contract, or get shorter, and, as a result, you kick the ball. Muscles move your body by contracting and then relaxing.

Next time you are rushing to get to class, remember how amazing it is that your body gets you there.

What other parts of the body do you know?
What do they do?
Which of these facts do you think are true?

a when you sleep, you grow 8mm
b human bone is as strong as stone
c the brain is our largest organ

16 **Look at 15. Read and choose the correct word.**

1 Bones, **muscles/brain** and joints are the three kinds of body parts that make up your musculoskeletal system.

2 Without your **organs/bones**, your body wouldn't have any shape.

3 Your joints connect two or more **nerves/bones** together.

4 By pulling your bones in different directions, your **muscles/joints** help your body move.

5 Muscles move your body by contracting and **playing/relaxing**.

6 When you want to move, your **nerves/joints** send messages to your muscles.

17 **Look at 15 and 16. Play a game with a partner.**

Without these, your body wouldn't have shape.

Bones! These move your body by contracting.

Um... nerves?

No. Muscles.

PROJECT

18 **Make an Amazing Body poster.**

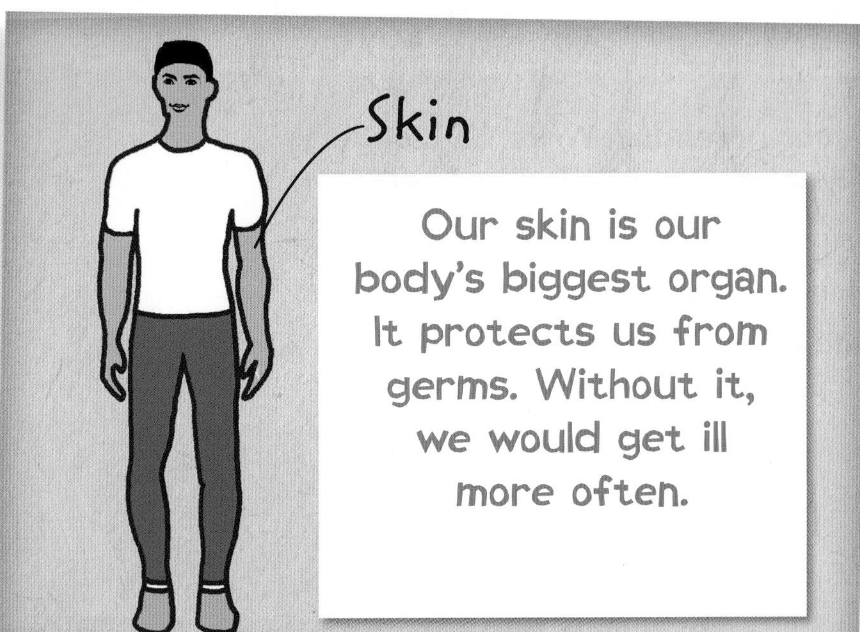

Without our skin, we would get ill more often.

3:48

19 **Listen and read. When did Aelita Andre start painting?**

Extraordinary Kids

There are some kids in the world who do things faster and better than most people. Take a look at some of these amazing kids.

Gregory Smith was born in 1990 in Keswick, Virginia, in the United States. Gregory could read before he was two years old. At ten, Gregory started attending university. By sixteen, Gregory had several university degrees. But he is more than just a genius. He travels the world trying to help young people everywhere. He hopes that he can help make the world a safer and more peaceful place for everyone.

At just eight years old, **Yuto Miyazawa** was already a professional musician! Yuto has already performed with music legends Ozzy Osbourne, Les Paul and G. E. Smith. He has appeared on several TV talk shows and performed at Madison Square Garden. Who knows what the future holds for this musical genius?

Many people in Australia are talking about an amazing young artist. **Aelita Andre** started showing her paintings when she was just three. Her father, a famous photographer, says that Aelita started to paint before her second birthday. Many people say that Aelita is too young to be considered a real artist. But her parents are still proud of her work.

Not everyone can be a genius but everyone has got his or her own special talents. What are yours?

20 **Read and write in your notebook. Write GS (Gregory Smith), YT (Yuto Miyazawa) or AA (Aelita Andre).**

1 He was a professional musician at eight years old.
2 She started showing paintings at three years old.
3 He had several university degrees by the age of sixteen.
4 Her father is a photographer.
5 He travels the world trying to help young people.
6 He has performed at Madison Square Garden.

BIG **Are you surprised by any of these stories? Which one? Why?**

21 **Read. Then match the parts of the review.**

body of review final sentence online name and date
rating title topic sentence

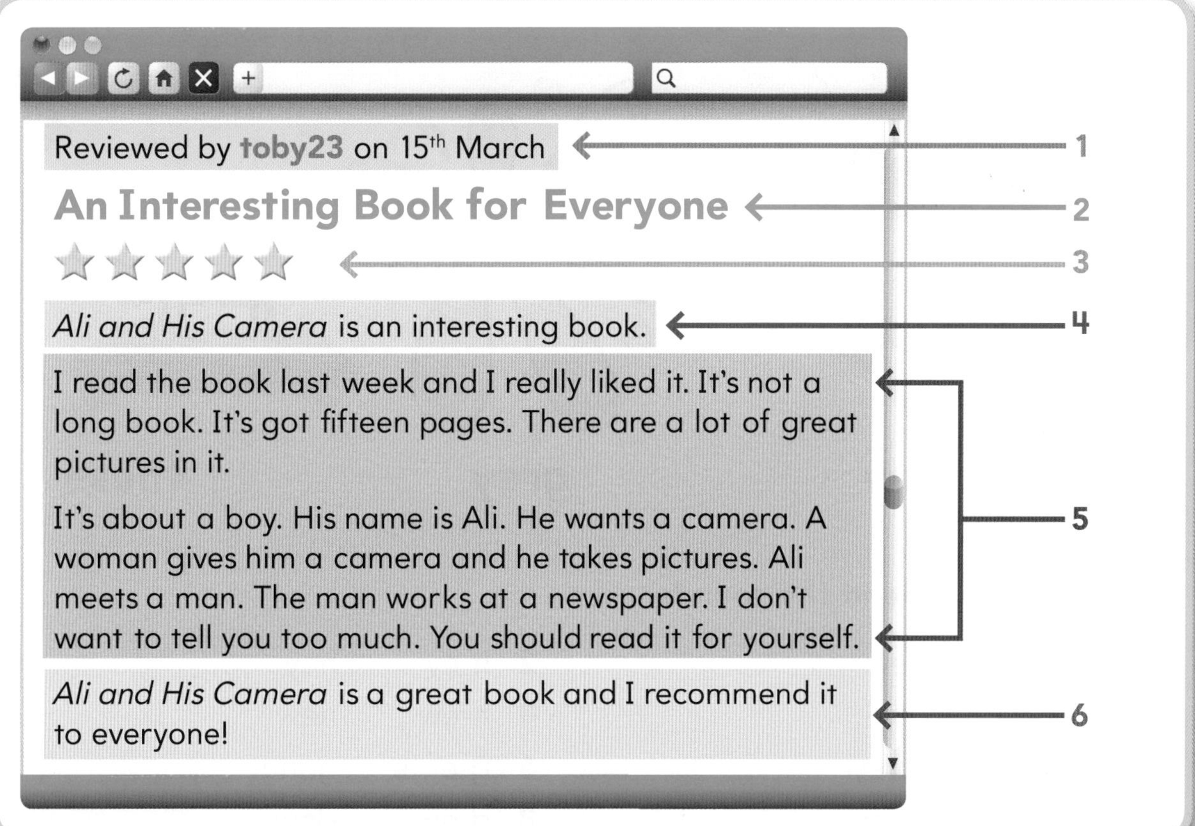

Writing Steps

22 **Write a review of a book or film you liked. Use the text in 21 to help you.**

1 Think of a book or film.
2 Make a list of what you liked about it.
3 Think of an online name and write today's date.
4 Write a title for your review.
5 Think of how many stars to give the book or film.
6 Write a topic sentence.
7 Write two paragraphs for the body of the review.
8 Write a final sentence.

3:49

23 Listen, read and repeat.

1 ew 2 ey 3 e_e

3:50

24 Listen and find. Then say.

3:51

25 Listen and blend the sounds.

1	f-ew	few	**2**	h-ey	hey
3	e-ve	eve	**4**	n-ew	new
5	p-r-ey	prey	**6**	g-e-ne	gene
7	th-ey	they	**8**	d-ew	dew

3:52

26 Read aloud. Then listen and chant.

These three are new!
They eat stew
And wear grey, too!

27 **Write the answers in your notebook.**

1 What does she think of making a website? (*amazing*)
2 What do they think of speaking Chinese? (*difficult*)
3 What does he think of drawing comic books? (*interesting*)
4 What do you think of playing badminton?

28 **Write the questions in your notebook.**

1 ? No, she doesn't know how to play the guitar.
2 ? Yes, they do. They're building a robot in school.
3 ? He'd like to learn how to snowboard.
4 ? I'd like to learn how to sing like a rock star.

29 **Complete for you. Then ask and answer.**

Know how to:

Don't know how to:

Would like to learn:

What I think about...:

Do you know how to...?

What do you think of...?

What would you like to learn how to do?

I Can

- **talk about things people know how to do.**
- **give opinions.**
- **describe how my body moves.**
- **write a review.**

How Well Do I Know It? Can I Use It?

1 **Think about it. Read and draw. Practise.**

☺ I know this. ☹ I need more practice. ☹ I don't know this.

		PAGES			
1	**Special days:** Earth Day, Father's Day, my parents' anniversary, New Year's Day...	84	☺	☹	☹
2	**Ways to celebrate:** give/get presents, have a party, watch fireworks, watch a parade...	84–85	☺	☹	☹
3	**Hobbies:** basketball, chess, coin collection, doll collection, shell collection, video games...	96	☺	☹	☹
4	**Talents:** bake a cake, build a robot, draw comic books, make a website, speak Chinese...	108	☺	☹	☹
5	When **are** you **going to** watch a parade? We**'re going to** watch a parade on New Year's Day. **Is** he **going to** give presents? Yes, he **is**./ No, he **isn't**. 1st – first, 10th – tenth, 20th – twentieth, 30th – thirtieth...	88–89	☺	☹	☹
6	Laura is a **good** chess player. Yoko is a **better** chess player **than** Laura. Alex is **the best** chess player in the class. I'm **good at** video games. She's **bad at** chess.	100–101	☺	☹	☹
7	**Do** you **know how to play** the piano? Yes, I **do**./No, I **don't**. What **would** she **like to learn how to do**? She**'d like to learn how to** sing. What **do** they **think of** snowboarding? They **think** it's dangerous.	112–113	☺	☹	☹

I Can Do It!

3:54 2 **Get ready.**

A Complete the dialogue. Use the correct form of the words in the box and a form of be going to. Then listen and check.

be (x2) dance do (x2) play sing skateboard

Samuel: Hey, [1]? you [2]? something for the school talent show on 9th May?

Melissa: I don't know. Maybe. Who [3]? in it?

Samuel: Well, Katie and Julia [4]? .

Melissa: Oh, wow. They're better dancers than I am.

Samuel: And Lucas [5]? .

Melissa: He's the best singer in the class! What else can I do?

Samuel: Let's see... Ricardo [6]? . He's very good at skateboarding. And Jen [7]? the guitar.

Melissa: Hey, I know what I can do!

Samuel: Great. What?

Melissa: I can catch food. Watch! [*Melissa throws some food and catches it in her mouth.*]

Melissa: [8]? anyone else [9]? that at the talent show?

Samuel: No, I don't think so.

Melissa: Excellent! I [10]? the best food catcher at the show!

B Practise the dialogue in **A** with a partner. Then practise again. Make up your own answers.

C Ask and answer the questions with a partner.

1 Why doesn't Melissa want to sing or dance in the talent show?

2 What special talents have you got? Explain.

Get set.

STEP 1 Make a poster for a school talent show. First, cut out the strips on page 125 of your Activity Book.

STEP 2 Glue the strips onto a sheet of paper or poster board.

STEP 3 Design your poster. Add your own pictures and text. Now you're ready to **Go!**

I think Leia's poster is the best one. It's got the coolest design!

4 Go!

A Hang up your posters around the classroom. Look at all the posters and vote on the best one.

B Make a sign-up sheet for your poster and hang it on the wall. Go around the class and sign up for five other talent shows. Choose a different talent for each one.

NAME	TALENT
Luisa	sing my favourite song
Celia	dance
Ricky	play the piano

C Compare sign-up sheets with your classmates. Work in a group. Tell the group what people are going to do in your talent show.

Ricky is going to play the piano at the talent show!

5 **Write about yourself in your notebook.**

- What do you usually do at parties?
- What do you do on school holidays?
- What are you going to do at the weekend?
- What hobbies or talents have you got?
- Do you like being in talent shows? Why/Why not?

All About Me

Date:__________

How Well Do I Know It Now?

6 A **Look at page 120 and your notebook. Draw again.**

B **Use a different colour.**

C **Read and think.**

I can ask my teacher for help.

I can practise.

7 **Rate this Checkpoint.**

very easy

easy

hard

very hard

fun

OK

not fun

Wordlist

Find these words in your language. Then write them in your notebook.

Unit 4	Page
allergies	44
cold	44
cough	44
cut	44
fever	44
headache	44
sneeze	44
sore throat	44
stomachache	44
toothache	44
feeling blue	45
himself	45
knee	45
rest	45
stay in bed	45
yourself	45
get upset	46
herself	46
plaster	46
blood	47
ketchup	47
napkin	47
medicine	48
stay up late	48
myself	49
ourselves	49
themselves	49
bacteria	50
fungi	50
germs	50
microscope	50
protozoa	50
toxins	50
virus	50
cure	52
boiled eggs	52
remedies	52
sunburn	52
vinegar	52
comma	53
knight	54
knock	54
knot	54
know	54
wrap	54
wreck	54
wrist	54
write	54
wrong	54

Unit 5	Page
Andean condor	56
angler fish	56
coconut crab	56
islands	56
population	56
tarsier	56
Tasmanian devil	56
thousands	56
volcanoes	56
volcano rabbit	56
wild	56
when	57
ago	58
chimpanzee (chimp)	58
endangered	58
million	58
tools	58
cheeky	59
destroy	59
habitat	59
joke	59
laughs	59
Asian elephants	60
black rhinos	60
komodo dragons	60
tigers	60
Andean flamingos	61
kill	61
polluted	61
pollution	61
bamboo	62
bumblebee bat	62
burn	62
cave	62
centimetre	62
China	62
Egyptian tortoise	62
extinct	62
Mexican walking fish	62
Mexico	62
moss	62
Myanmar	62
Nepal	62
red panda	62
stream	62
Thailand	62
Egypt	63
breathe	64
continent	64
dragon	64
extinction	64
monster	64
mythical	64
exclamation mark	65
full stop	65
question mark	65
dolphin	66
phantom	66
phone	66
photo	66
whale	66
wheat	66
wheel	66

Unit 6	Page
by hand	68
coal stove	68
electric lights	68
horse and carriage	68
microwave	68
mobile phone	68
mp3	68
operator	68
oil lamp	68
radio	68
washing machine	68
pump	69
tap	69
channel	70
remote control	70
modern	71
technology	71
average speed	74
distance travelled	74
equation	74
hours	74
how far	74
kilometres per hour	74
ancestor	76
culture	76
nomadic	76
traditional	76
tundra	76
age	78
badge	78
bridge	78
cage	78
edge	78
fridge	78
hedge	78
large	78
page	78
sponge	78

Unit 7	Page
Earth Day	84
Father's Day	84
Midsummer's Day	84
New Year's Day/Eve	84
parents' anniversary	84
School Sports' Day	84
cheer	85
give/get a card	85
give/get presents	85
have a party	85
treat	85
watch fireworks	85
wear different clothes	85
watch a parade	85
celebrate	86
right	87
wrong	87
feast	90
festival	90
fight	90
glacier	90
guests	90
messy	90
powder	90
leap year	92
lucky	92
unlucky	92
email address	93
greeting	93
signature	93
blue	94
cube	94
cute	94
duke	94
glue	94
huge	94
nature	94
picture	94
treasure	94
true	94

Unit 8	Page
coin collection	96
doll collection	96
shell collection	96
toy car collection	96
good at	97
character	98
my	100
bad at	101
by	102
croquet	102
employer	102
fabric	102
marbles	102
needle and thread	102
stitches	102
rules	102
underwater	104
closing	105
date	105
informal letter	105
light	106
night	106
right	106
sky	106
try	106

Unit 9	Page
bake a cake	108
build a robot	108
draw comic books	108
hip-hop artist	108
make a website	108
new	108
play badminton	108
sing like a rock star	108
snowboard	108
speak Chinese	108
amazing	109
boring	109
cool	109
dangerous	109
difficult	109
interesting	109
they	110
contract	114
joint	114
nerve	114
organ	114
relax	114
system	114
these	114
extraordinary	116
perform	116
professional	116
online name	117
rating	117
review	117
chew	118
eve	118
few	118
gene	118
grey	118
hey	118
prey	118
stew	118

Base Form	Simple Past
ask	asked
bake	baked
be	was/were
begin	began
bring	brought
build	built
buy	bought
call	called
catch	caught
celebrate	celebrated
change	changed
come	came
cook	cooked
cut	cut
destroy	destroyed
do	did
draw	drew
drink	drank
drive	drove
eat	ate
explain	explained
fall	fell
feed	fed
feel	felt
fight	fought
find	found
fly	flew
get	got
give	gave
go	went
grow	grew
have	had
hear	heard
help	helped
hit	hit
hold	held
hope	hoped
keep	kept
kill	killed
know	knew
learn	learned
leave	left
like	liked
listen	listened
live	lived
look	looked
lose	lost
love	loved
make	made

Base Form	Simple Past
meet	met
move	moved
need	needed
perform	performed
plan	planned
play	played
put	put
read	read
realize	realized
rest	rested
ride	rode
ring	rang
run	ran
say	said
see	saw
sell	sold
send	sent
sing	sang
sit	sat
skateboard	skateboarded
sleep	slept
snowboard	snowboarded
speak	spoke
stand	stood
start	started
stay up	stayed up
swim	swam
take	took
talk	talked
tell	told
think	thought
throw	threw
travel	travelled
try	tried
turn	turned
understand	understood
use	used
visit	visited
wait	waited
wake up	woke up
walk	walked
want	wanted
wash	washed
watch	watched
wear	wore
worry	worried
write	wrote
yell	yelled

3:55 3:56 Big English Song

From the mountaintops to the bottom of the sea,
From a big blue whale to a baby bumblebee –
If you're big, if you're small, you can have it all
And you can be anything you want to be!

It's bigger than you. It's bigger than me.
There's so much to do and there's so much to see!
The world is big and beautiful and so are we!
Think big! Dream big! Big English!

So in every land, from the desert to the sea
We can all join hands and be one big family.
If we love, if we care, we can go anywhere!
The world belongs to everyone; it's ours to share.

It's bigger than you. It's bigger than me.
There's so much to do and there's so much to see!
The world is big and beautiful and so are we!
Think big! Dream big! Big English!

It's bigger than you. It's bigger than me.
There's so much to do and there's so much to see!
The world is big and beautiful and waiting for me.
A one, two, three...
Think big! Dream big! Big English!

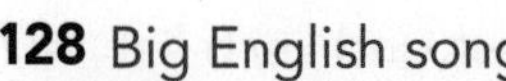